S0-CLE-001

EXURBS:
URBAN RESIDENTIAL
DEVELOPMENTS IN
THE COUNTRYSIDE

Dinker I. Patel

University Press
of America™

Copyright © 1980 by

University Press of America, Inc.
P.O. Box 19101, Washington, DC 20036

ISBN: 0-8191-1001-9 **(Case)**
ISBN: 0-8191-1002-7 **(Perfect)**

Library of Congress Catalog Card Number: 79-48040

To Mother:
Shantaben Ishwarbhai Patel

ACKNOWLEDGEMENTS

The author acknowledges the interest, enthusiasm, and cooperation of many people in the preparation of this book. In particular, I wish to acknowledge my debt to Wilford Bladen, Thomas Field, Charles Humphrey, Glenda Lynch, Pravin Patel, Julius Pauer, Phil Phillips, Karl Raitz and Gerald Slatin.

Previous studies provide the basis upon which other research is conducted . This study is no exception, therefore, the authors whose works are reviewed and or cited in this publication, deserve a special note of thanks. Appreciation is also expressed to all the exurbanites whose responses made it possible to gain insights into their lifestyles. The subdivision developers, planners and local governmental officials who willingly gave their time and information also deserve my sincere gratitude.

CONTENTS

LIST OF TABLES

LIST OF ILLUSTRATIONS

x

PREFACE

In recent years many Americans have opted to
live beyond the suburbs in islands of exurban de-
development. The distinctive exurban settlement pattern that is evolving beyond the traditional geographic city is the subject of this research.

In this study the term *exurb* is defined as a
discrete, areally organized subdivision with an internal street pattern, located in a rural setting.
It is located far enough beyond the frontier of suburban development that it will not be engulfed by the
expanding city within the forseeable future, and
thus is an urban island in a rural setting.

Three broad themes - the process of exurban development, the pattern of exurban distribution, and
the socioeconomic characteristics and residential
preferences of the exurbanites - were explored to
gain insights into the exurban phenomenon that has
recently been superimposed on the stable, culturally
rich and picturesque landscape of the Kentucky Bluegrass.

The process of conversion of rural land to exurban residential use involves many decisions: the
decision of the predevelopment landowner to sell or
hold his land; the decision of the residential developer to invest in a suburban or exurban site, and
the individual households to live in a suburb or an
exurb.

The private developer of an exurb must use a
systematic step-by-step process which includes the
acquisition of land for subdivision, preliminary
and final approval of a land subdivision plat by the
local planning and zoning commission (if one exists),
the county engineer and utility company representatives. The approved plat is then recorded with the
appropriate county clerk's office. Small exurbs with
up to twenty-five lots are usually developed as a
single unit. However, in the larger subdivisions a
parcel-by-parcel development process is followed.

The following questions related to the distribution and nature of exurbs were posed:

(1) What is the areal distribution and extent of exurbs?

(2) Do exurbs vary in their physical quality?

(3) What are the socioeconomic characteristics and residential preferences of the exurbanites?

To answer the first question, field reconnaissance was undertaken to locate the exurbs in the Bluegrass study area. The result was a map of the areal distribution of exurbs. The mapped distribution of exurbs was found to be closely oriented to the well established, relatively dense highway network in the study area.

The overall exurban distributional pattern of the one hundred exurbs found in the study area was used as the basis of a locational model of exurbs. Four distinct zones were identified in the model. They were *zone one* the geographic city, which extends to the edge of the contiguous suburbs; *zone two*, comprising of non-urban land uses and urban exclaves; *zone three*, in which exurbs are located, lying beyond the frontier of urban development in the forseeable future but within the commuting range of the city; and *zone four*, an area of open space and farmscape beyond the commuting range of the city. The exurban model was modified to show the influence of smaller urban centers and radial transportation routes, which produce a greater extent of urban development and a higher density of exurbs.

The second question examined in this study was posed as a hypothesis--exurbs vary in their physical quality among the counties of the study area. A quality rating scale, which classified each exurb in one of six categories was developed and applied to each exurb. The classification was based on an overall rating which took into consideration such exurban attributes as the type, value and condition of housing; the quality of streets; and overall residential area appearance. A cross tabulation of the number of dwellings and exurbs for each county by exurban quality rating showed that exurbs vary in their physical quality among the counties of the study area. This variation results from differences in zoning regulations, subdivision standards and the developer's perception of the housing market.

A survey of selected exurban communities was undertaken to determine the socioeconomic status (SES) characteristics and residential preferences of the exurbanites. An examination of the income, education, and occupational levels of the exurbanites revealed that--contrary to the commonly perpetuated myth of the exurbs having exclusively high SES values--individual exurbs vary in their predominant SES characteristics. Exurbanites preferred living in their countryside subdivision because of open space, a close to nature environment, and peaceful, quiet, and safe surroundings. Being close to work was relatively less important to the exurbanites than the other amenities. Questions related to the residential move history of the exurbanites substantiated the hypothesis that most exurbanites have made their residential move from suburbs and central cities to exurbs.

Suggestions for guiding exurban growth include comprehensive long-range land use controls, multi-county planning, and the establishment of subdivision standards to eliminate the unequal development standards which exist between counties on the one hand and between urban and exurban developments on the other.

From the consumer point of view this study can serve in the decision process concerning exurban living. The findings of this study can be applied to the personal perception of the amenities and disamenities of an exurban residential location.

1. INTRODUCTION

In recent years an increasing number of Americans have chosen to live beyond the suburbs of large and medium size cities in planned residential subdivisions or exurbs. Exurban development is particularly visible in the rural fringe beyond the contiguous suburbs of Lexington, Kentucky, which has experienced rapid growth in its population in recent decades. Thus the Bluegrass Region of Kentucky, with Lexington at its center, offers the setting within which the exurban phenomenon is examined. For the purpose of this study the term *exurb* is defined as a discrete subdivision areally organized on an internal street pattern, and located in a rural setting far enough beyond the frontier of suburban development that it will not be engulfed by the expanding city within the foreseeable future. It is an urban island in a rural setting. The residents of the exurbs will be considered *exurbanitos* regardless of their place of work or previous residence. Exurbs are organized developments which involve the conversion of rural land to residential sites to accommodate the housing needs and aspirations of a broad socioeconomic spectrum of automobile oriented Americans who have chosen a life style that does not fit the mold of central cities, suburbs, or satellite cities. Most of the exurbs in the Lexington *compage* or the Bluegrass region of Central Kentucky have developed since World War II. This new residential frontier is the subject of this study.

Preliminary work on the research topic suggests three broad themes which need to be explored to gain insights into the locational characteristics of the exurbs which now create urban islands over the picturesque landscape of central Kentucky. Only organized exurbs, i.e. those with an internal street system, will be included in the study. This study focused upon three themes.

1. *The development of exurbs.* The process of exurban development was examined by analyzing data from subdivision plats and interviews.

1

The role of land developers, planning and
zoning officials, realtors and the buyers
of residential property was evaluated to
gain insights into the process of exurban
growth.

2. *The distribution of exurbs.* The pattern of
exurban distribution was examined in terms
of site attributes and characteristics of
relative location. The number, size,
quality, and temporal growth of exurbs are
additional variables which will be useful
in analyzing the regional as well as county
to county variations in the exurban devel-
opmental pattern.

3. *Survey of exurbanites.* This focus of the study
may be stated in the form of a question:--
What are the; (a) residential preferences
and; (b) socioeconomic characteristics of
the exurbanites?

A survey of the exurbanites was conducted to
gain insights into their residential choices and
socioeconomic characteristics. The type of questions
and the sampling design will be discussed under methodology in chapter four.

While the study area used in this research is
limited to Kentucky's Bluegrass Region (See Page 8),
exurban phenomena is by no means restricted to this
locality. The development of exurbs in the United
States in terms of overall population trends and
changes in urban morphology will be discussed before
outlining the locational characteristics of the
study area.

Population Trends and Changes in Urban Morphology

Over 60 percent of Amercians lived in rural
areas at the turn of the century but since that
time the proportion has declined. This decline
in the population of rural areas reached a mile-
stone in 1920, when for the first time, over half
the United States population enumerated lived in
urban areas. Each succeeding census reports an
increase in the size of the American population

and the proportion of the American population that was urban.[2] In 1970, 68 percent of the 203,210,158 people in the United States lived in urban areas.[3] Through time, urban areas have undergone changes. The nineteenth century cities were compact compared to the twentieth century cities. The latter have expanded at their fringes, resulting in the development of suburbs. A larger proportion of population now lives in suburban portions of the Standard Metropolitan Statistical Areas (S.M.S.A.'s) (37.2 percent) than in either the central cities of SMSA's (31.4 percent) or in areas outside SMSA's (31.4 percent).[4] As Sylvia Fava recently wrote:

> The United States is already a nation in which suburbanites constitute the largest portion but not yet the majority of Americans. Many of these suburbanites will be suburban-born and bred, rather than having decentralized from the center city. Their moves will be from suburb to suburb or suburb to exurb, and they will thus have little direct life experience with high density living and central city problems.[5]

There were 84,765,360 Americans living outside urbanized areas in 1970 of which 45,591,154 or 22.4 percent of the national population were rural non-farm dwellers, a category roughly equivalent to exurbanites. (See Table 1).

Some general aspects of urban, suburban and exurban development are reviewed to provide a framework for this study. The inner city in the United States has become the home of unassimilated minorities. Increasingly, the middle and upper class have fled the city and see the inner city only through the windows of commuter trains and from automobiles passing along expressways and arterial streets.[6] The expansion of the suburban sector of the urban population has resulted in the flattening of the urban population density gradient outward from the city center.[7] Population shifts toward the edges of the city have been followed by the suburbanization of business and industry so that "the critical mass of American society is now external to the [central]city".[8]

TABLE 1

POPULATION OF THE UNITED STATES BY PLACE OF RESIDENCE

Location	Total	Percentage of United States Population	Percentage of Population Inside Urbanized Areas	Percentage of Rural Population
United States	203,211,926	100.00		
Inside Urbanized areas	118,446,566	58.29	100.00	
Inside central cities	63,921,648	31.46	53.97	
Outside central cities	54,524,882	26.83	46.03	
Outside urbanized areas	84,765,360	41.71		
Rural	53,878,039	26.51		100.00
Farm	8,286,885	4.08		15.38
Non-farm	45,591,154	22.44		84.62

Source: U.S. Bureau of the Census, U.S. Census of Population: 1970, Number of Inhabitants. Final Report PC(1)-A1, Washington, D.C.: U.S. Government Printing Office, 1971.

4

The change in urban population densities may be related to developments in transportation since changes in the mode of transportation open up new residential areas. Adams[9] has recognized four transportation eras:

1. The walking/horse era: to the 1880's
2. The electric streetcar era: 1880's to World War I
3. The recreational auto era: 1920's to 1941
4. The freeway era: post-World War II

During each transportation period residential growth took a different spatial form. The first and third eras produced a somewhat restrictive and generally zonal form of growth. The second and fourth eras led to radial growth along streetcar lines or in the direction of the axes of urban freeways accompanied by lower density gradients. In the United States the streetcar, the commuter railway and especially the automobile revolutionized urban structure by reducing the cost and time required for travel.[10]

The development of an efficient transportation system has also contributed to the changing American landscapes. With the completion of the majority of the Interstate System the open country has been transformed into "corridor cities".[11] The movement beyond the traditional "suburban" to exurban areas has resulted in residential sites that are further from the central city and where population densities are relatively lower. Consequently the "twentieth century metropolises have so burst their nineteenth century boundaries that...a network of Daily Urban Systems (DUS's), each with a radius of 75-80 miles, now blankets all except the most sparsely settled parts of the country, embracing daily activities and travel of ninety [sic] percent of the nation's population".[12] Indeed, commuting has become an indispensable part of the American life style.

The widespread desire for life in rural areas and small towns over that of the metropolitan city on the part of many Americans may be attributed to a "growing sense of increasing urban problems of pollution, crime, congestion, social alienations, and other real or suspected effects of large-scale

massing of people." Furthermore the developments
of the 1960's "...the environmental-ecological
movement, the youth revolution with its somewhat
antimaterialistic and antisuburban component, and
the narrowing of traditional urban-rural gaps in
conditions of life all seem to have contributed
to the movement to non-metro areas".[13] Additional
insights into rural versus urban living preferences
are provided by Phillips in a recent study on
exurban commuters:

> Many forces have cojoined to make life
> in outwardly rural surroundings an attractive
> alternative to many Americans: greater mobil-
> ity, shorter work hours, higher wages, and
> desire to escape the crowding and dangers
> of the city. An even more important factor
> may have been the development of a "rural
> mystique" in which the city is seen as
> crowded, hectic, dangerous and dirty, while
> rural areas are seen as being open, tranquil,
> safe, and clean.[14]

Urban growth results in substantial amounts
of land being converted from agricultural and
other rural uses to urban uses. Nationally, about
4,000 acres of agricultural land are converted to
urban uses daily.[15] Although estimates of urban
encroachment on the rual land vary, the amount
of land so preempted is not as critical as manag-
ing the conversion of rural land to residential
sites.[16]

The process of settlement reviewed thus far
may be summarized in terms of broad trends and
dynamic changes. During the nineteenth century
the American population was predominantly rural.
However, it was a period of rapid shift of population toward the city. In time the compact
nineteenth century city underwent suburban expansion. More recently some urban Americans have
moved beyond the suburbs to islands of exurban
development. These exurbs are the product of
imaginative private developers capitalizing
on the desire of the consuming public to live
in the country by offering them alternaive
residential environments to central city and
suburban living.

The study area comprises seven Kentucky counties -- Bourbon, Clark, Fayette, Jessamine, Madison, Scott, and Woodford (See Fig. 1), which are approximately coincident with the physiographic region of the Inner Bluegrass.[17] In this study the term *Bluegrass Region* or *Inner Bluegrass* will be used to refer to the seven county area described above. In recent years the Inner Bluegrass Region has made substantial gains in economic development and growth of population (See Table 2). Two generations that can be drawn from Table 2 are: firstly, that all the study area counties are experiencing growth in their population and parallel growth in other sectors of the economy; and secondly, that there are variations between counties in their growth rates. For example, the population change for the period 1950-74 in Fayette county was 85.5 percent, compared to Jessamine county's 69.4 percent and Bourbon county's 5.3 percent. Most of Fayette county's growth was on the south side of the city of Lexington. Jessamine county, which is located to the south and adjacent to Fayette, experienced growth through the development of residential communities oriented to Lexington. In contrast, the north half of Fayette county and adjacent Bourbon county have experienced relatively less growth because of restrictive zoning of farm land which has limited urban expansion to the north. The economic well-being, and the greater range of mobility provided by the automobile, and accessibility via improved transportation routes, have greatly increased the residential location choices of Kentuckians and indeed all Americans in the last quarter century.

The foregoing factors have contributed to a distinctive exurban settlement pattern around many American cities which has not yet been rigorously studied.

Dispersed across the gently rolling Bluegrass plain are about one hundred organized residential subdivisions or exurbs. Two limestone posts and a name sign usually mark the entrance and exit to the exurbs (See Fig. 2). Dwellings are usually

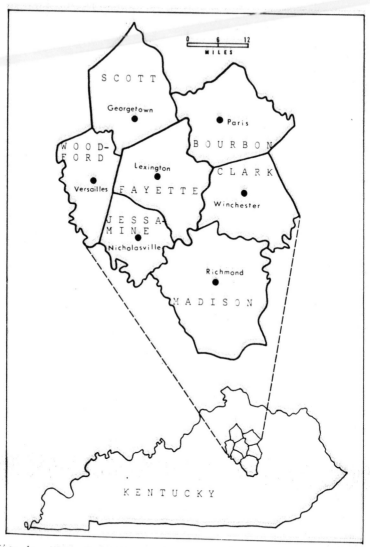

Fig. 1. Kentucky's Bluegrass Region: Seven County Study Area.

8

TABLE 2

CHANGE IN POPULATION AND SELECTED SECTORS OF THE
ECONOMY IN KENTUCKY'S INNER BLUEGRASS REGION

County	Population 1950[a]	Population 1970[a]	Estimated population 1974[b]	Population change 1950-74 (percentage)	Rural Non-farm population 1970[a] (percentage)	Urban population 1970[c] (percentage)	Value added by manufacture 1972[c] (millions of dollars)	Change in value added by manufacture, 1963-72[c] (percentage)	Retail trade sales, 1972	Change in retail trade sales, 1963-72[d] (percentage)
Bourbon	17,752	18,476	18,700	5.3	32.4	42.3	8.5	73.5	26.1	23.1
Clark	18,898	24,090	25,600	35.5	26.2	55.6	80.8	536.2	50.8	107.3
Fayette	100,746	174,323	186,900	85.5	5.7	91.7	417.7	162.2	504.6	119.9
Jessamine	12,458	17,430	21,100	69.4	28.8	53.1	3.4	41.7	23.1	87.8
Madison	31,179	42,730	46,200	48.2	30.1	55.7	41.4	177.9	79.3	120.3
Scott	15,141	17,948	18,400	21.5	29.5	43.1	33.4	131.9	25.6	91.0
Woodford	11,212	14,432	15,600	28.8	40.6	39.3	60.8	232.2	20.2	62.9

Sources:
[a] U.S. Bureau of the Census, County and City Data Book, 1972, A Statistical Abstract Supplement, Washington, D.C.: U.S. Government Printing Office, 1973.

[b] U.S. Department of Commerce, Current Population Reports, Series P-26, No. 120, Washington, D.C.: U.S. Government Printing Office, June, 1975, pp.3-5.

[c] U.S. Bureau of the Census, Census of Manufacturers, 1963,1972. Area Statistics, Washington, D.C.: U.S. Government Printing Office, 1966, 1975.

[d] U.S. Bureau of the Census, Census of Business, 1963,1972. Area Statistics, Washington, D.C.: U.S. Government Printing Office, 1966, 1975.

Fig. 2 Name Signs Mark the Entrance to an Exurb

located on a gridiron or "vermicular" street pattern with several short cul-de-sacs. The number of
dwellings per exurb range from fewer than ten to
more than two hundred.

A variety of terms are used to name exurbs.
About one-fourth of the exurbs have names which include the descriptive term "estate". Other terms
frequently used are: "hills", "heights", "manor",
"village", "woods", and "green". These names con-
note an image of exclusivity, or closeness to the
natural environment. The home owner's preference
for exurban living, and their desire to think that
they are in contact with nauture, is thus recognized by some developers who give exurbs names
such as Forest Grove, Rolling Hills, Greenbrier
Estates, Lakewood and Lee's Park.

The national trend in areal residential shift
from the central city to the suburb and from
suburb to exurb was examined in the first section
of this chapter. The second section is devoted
to a review of the literature, definitions and
usages of the exurban concept, and a typology of
Bluegrass settlements.

Chapter Two is devoted to an examination of
the process of exurban development, while the
pattern of exurban distribution in Kentucky's
Bluegrass is discussed in the third chapter. The
results of the field survey conducted to gain
insights into the residential choices and socioeconomic characteristics of the exurbanites are the
subject of the fourth chapter. The overall findings
of the research are summarized in chapter five,
which also includes recommendations for further
studies.

LITERATURE REVIEW

The settlement pattern of exurban development
in the Bluegrass is not unique. A survey of the
literature has revealed the following generalizations about exurbs:

1. There is no explicit definition of exurbs
developed in previous geographic literature.

2. There is no existing study which specifically addressed the development, distribution, socioeconomic characteristics and residential preferences of exurbanites.

3. The studies that have some bearing on the current research are found among a variety of disciplines including sociology, economics, geography, political science and psychology. These studies deal with such diverse topics as urban sprawl, suburbanization, the rural-urban fringe, land use, zoning regulations, planned development, leap-frog development, land economics, environmental quality and commuting behavior.

Studies that focus on the various aspects of the urban and particularly exurban development processes, the resultant spatial pattern and the characteristics of the exurbanites will be reviewed here.

Definitions of an Exurb

The term "exurb" was coined by Auguste C. Spectorsky,[18] an author and editor, whose publication, *The Exurbanites*, is the only extensive study on the subject. Although not a scholarly work the book offers many insights into the exurban phenomena and the personality of the exurbanites who are distinguished from urbanites, suburbanites, and ruralites. To Spectorsky,

The word 'exurb' (and its derivates 'exurban' and 'exurbanite') carries no connotation of something that has ceased to be, of something in the past; rather what is intended is a clarification of something extra that has characterized the journey of the exurbanite, out and away from the city, in a wistful search for roots for the realization of a dream, for a home.[19]

The exurbanites Spectorsky wrote about in 1955 lived in Connecticut, New York, and Pennsylvania and were tied to jobs in the communications trade in New York City. Their place of residence was "further from New York than the suburbs on the same railway line. Its (the exurban) houses are more widely spaced and generally more various and more expensive. The town center tends to quaintness and class, rather than modernity and glass, and the further one lives from the (commuter railroad) station the better."[20]

Webster's New World Dictionary defines an exurb as:

> A region, generally semi-rural, beyond the suburbs of a city, inhabited largely by persons in the upper income group;

and an exurbanite as:

> a person living in an exurb; especially one commuting to the city as a business or professional person.[21]

Maurice H. Yeates and Barry J. Garner define exurbs as: "settlements beyond and spatially distinct from the immediate environs of the urban area."[22] They noted that after 1864 there was a rapid growth in railroad towns, such as Burlingame, San Mateo, San Carlos, Belmont, and Atherton in the San Francisco area which "were among the location of the wealthy who gained their livelihood in the city."[23] The impact of the railroad on urban structure and form was further stressed.

> Thus the railroad contributed to a further spatial stratification of society in that the wealthiest of all were now permitted (if they so chose) to live at considerable distances from the urban area yet maintain their vital social contacts and daily business interests in the central part of the city. The pattern of growth resulting from the influence of the railroads was quite restrictive for it could only occur in nucleations along the radial lines of the railroad companies.[24]

13

In a more recent study, James E. Vance, Jr., indicated that throughout their history Americans living in the city have looked upon the countryside as a place for a specialized form of urban settlement and that the paramount reason for this is the "search for the image of the good life not the second best or the comprise, but the ideal in the mind of the searcher."[25]

Discussing the morphology of the urban countryside, as typified ny the northeastern Megalopolis,[26] Vance distinguished between commuting exurbia and periodic exurbia; the former involving a daily "radial journey from the city", and the latter encompassing the "interstices between those prongs of city life",[27] where writers, painters and others who work "at home" and need only infrequent ties with the central cities live. The attitudes and designs of the exurbanites "have shaped a very distinctive rural landscape, an urban pastoralism, which has given Megalopolis its unique quality."[28]

The studies reviewed thus far clearly point to the urban origin of the exurban settlement. In another recent study, the noted land economist, Marion Clawson, identified the suburb as "an integral though outlying part of the urban complex to which it is physically adjacent,"[29] whereas:

> The term "exurbia" has come to be applied to a less clearly defined type of land use and of living, more remote from the city and less closely integrated with it. There is no sharp, clear line between rather remote suburb and relatively near exurbia, or between suburban living loosely oriented to the city and exurban living much less dependent upon the central city. But exurbia, as a present land use and as a possibility for the future clearly deserves some attention in consideration of urban impact upon rural countryside.[30]

Clawson noted that many exurban residences start out as vacation places but later become year-round retirement homes. With rising real incomes, more people in retirement can afford to live where they choose, and perhaps in further rebellion against

urban and suburban living, exurban living can be
expected to increase in importance and in its
impact on rural countryside.[31]

One generalization that can be drawn from the
foregoing definitions is that exurbia in its various
forms and collective definitions has become an
accepted concept, which, however, does not seem to
have received the scholarly attention or careful
definition that urban and suburban areas have been
accorded. Exurbia represents a distinctive settlement frontier on the rural landscape.[32]

Another generalization from the literature
review suggests that exurbs are the residential
abodes of only the wealthy. This research will show
that the exurbanites in the Bluegrass range along a
continuum from low to high in their socioeconomic
characteristics. Because there are variations in the
type of settlements an attempt will be made to examine the morphologically discrete types of rural
nonfarm settlements including exurbs in the Bluegrass
Region of Kentucky.

EXURBS IN THE CONTEXT OF
BLUEGRASS SETTLEMENT TYPES

In order to determine the place of exurbs in
the broader context of Bluegrass settlement types
and patterns this section reviews five studies of
Bluegrass settlement types, authored by Oscar Rucker,
Jr.,[34] the Lexington-Fayette County Planning Commission,[35] Peter C. Smith,[36] Thomas P. Field,[37]
and Phillip D. Phillips,[38] which deal with some
aspect of nucleated settlements in Kentucky including rural settlements in general, Negro hamlets,
mobile home parks, and exurban communities. A
review of these studies will be followed by the
identification of five morphologically distinct
settlement types including exurbs, in Kentucky's
Bluegrass.

Previous Studies

The objective of Oscar Rucker's study was to
identify the physical and functional characteristics

15

of rural settlement clusters in Madison County, Kentucky. With regard to the location of the nucleated settlements he notes:

> The choice of rural settlement cluster sites may be influenced by a variety of factors. Such factors include the natural resources of the area, the current method of transportation and communication, the physical landscape and the cultural traditions of the local population. The passage of time may alter most of these factors so as to favor the continued development of the site, to hold its development at a status quo or to completely eliminate the development from the landscape.[39]

Rucker's field reconnaissance revealed forty-three settlement clusters of which one was a village, thirty were hamlets, ten were rural residential clusters, and two were what he termed "rural subdivisions". He identified hamlets using an earlierdefinition devised by Glenn Trewartha in a study of Wisconsin settlements where,

> "to be classed as a hamlet, a rural set-cluster must consist of at least five residential structures or other buildings used for commercial or cultural purposes, clustered within one-quarter mile, and it must contain at least one but not more than nine retail and service units."[40]

Rucker also used the precedent established by Trewartha in identifying places with more than five residential structures and nine retail and service units as "villages."

Clustered places without retail establishments that could not qualify as either hamlet or village were designed as "rural residential cluster" or simply "rural subdivision" by Rucker. He describes a rural subdivision as a "new settlement pattern" which had arisen because of "recent improvements in transportation, communication, and domestic utilities coupled with the personal preferences of residents who desire lower taxes and a country atmosphere".[41] This description is adequate to define an exurb as synonymous to his rural subdivision.

The Lexington-Fayette County Planning Commission report *Rural Settlements Housing Study* identified five groups of settlements in Fayette county:

1. Early historic settlements, such as Cross Roads (Athens) Cleveland (Clays Ferry) and Spearsville (spears), which made their appearance before the end of the Eighteenth Century.

2. Small farms close together which formed into settlements, for example, Loradale and Shannondale. These have been white communities throughout their existence.

3. Communities formed before the Civil War by land owners who subdivided land on the edge of their estates for some of their slaves to live close to work.

4. Communities formed by large land owners but established after the Civil War.

5. Communities established during the first half of this century as a result of property owners in the rural areas subdividing their land for home sites.

A total of seventeen settlements, all established by 1950, fell within the five groups of settlements outlined above.

The Planning Commission Study included an inventory of population, land use, housing characteristics and services available to the rural settlements. Next, the study considered certain constraints on planning activity, such as cost factors, local development policy, sanitary sewer disposal policy and government structural differences. These constraints, when considered with the population and housing characteristics of the rural settlements, led to four general planning alternatives: retaining the status quo, area

17

wide redevelopment, limited development and rehabili-
tation, and relocation into the urban area.

These alternatives follow two basic principles.
"One was to phase out the rural communities by allow-
ing the existing trends of depopulation to continue
or to encourage the process by extending relocation
assistance. The second principle was to correct the
housing deficiencies in the communities thus perpetu-
ating their existence. The plan recommended that the
second of these alternatives be followed where no
critical health or safety hazards exist.[42]

Finally, an important feature of the Planning
Commission Study was a land use profile of each
settlement which included information on the history,
population characteristics, the nature and use of
the land, and the quality of buildings, public services, plan recommendations and a detailed land use map.

The third settlement study, by Peter C. Smith,
was an investigation of the Negro settlement pattern
in the Bluegrass Region.

The author identified twenty-nine Negro hamlets
about which he comments:

To a remarkable degree this settlement pattern and certain vestiges of its social structure
are still intact in the Bluegrass. The Negro
dwellings have been removed from the immediate
vicinity of the large estate mansion, and are
now clustered out of view on the back of the
property. The Negroes in most cases now own
their own home and the small garden plot ac-
companying it. Yet many are directly dependent
upon the estates for employment, thereby maintaining an occupational relationship that may
well be over three hundred years old.[43]

Smith defined Negro hamlets as "small rural
clusters of houses where Negroes are numerically
dominant (or where Negroes were numerically dominant
in the past)".[44] He cited the circumstances which
led to the establishment of this particular type of
settlement in the Bluegrass. Fifteen of the twenty-
nine hamlets were established when land was sold or

given to the Negroes, upon emancipation, by local estate owners and former slave holders. Three hamlets originated when "land was purchased by a 'developer' for the express purpose of selling lots to Negroes at a profit."[45] Four hamlets were formed through what the author called "unique chain of events." Finally, seven hamlets were listed as having been formed by "a combination of the above conditions."[46]

The fact that Negro hamlets were located on the back of Bluegrass estates, usually on a dead end lane or in some inconspicious place led Smith to compare the twenty-nine Negro hamlets in his study with a sample of thirty-eight white hamlets, and conclude that there is indeed a significant difference between the accessibility of the Negro hamlets and the white hamlets.[47]

Further comparisons of the black versus white hamlets by Smith on housing and employment revealed that:

"...the quality of housing in the Negro hamlets is substantially below that of the white hamlets." "...a much higher percentage of the whites held urban type jobs" (75 percent compared to 40 percent for blacks), also..."more than nineteen percent of the Negroes interviewed were actively employed on the large estates of the Bluegrass while none of the whites was so employed."[48]

The study by Thomas P. Field examined the areal distribution of mobile homes at two levels. The first part was a statewide analysis based on secondary data sources and utilizing the one hundred twenty counties of Kentucky as the units of analysis.[49] The second part was a position report regarding the distribution of mobile homes based on field reconnaissance of the seven Bluegrass counties centered on Lexington.

Of particular interest to the present study is Field's identification of mobile home parks in the rural areas of Bluegrass which form a specific type of nucleated settlement or exurb. Also of interest is his recognition of the relatively recent origin of the mobile home park. The average date of origin of a representative park was 1960.[50]

In his study Field states that "the unevenness of the individual county growth of mobile home proportions can readily be attributed to the interplay of timing of economic events with the timing of town and county zoning actions",[51] which are illustrated by citing specific instances in the spatial parameters of mobile home location. Field concludes that in terms of economy, efficiency and the degree of owner commitment the residential mobile home has no standard dwelling counterpart.[52]

The study by Phillip D. Phillips examined the significance of commuting from rural to urban areas. In introducing the subject the author points out that "the long strings of houses along country roads, the mobile home parks, and the subdivisions in many parts of Kentucky attest to the importance of exurban commuting in the state."[53]

Phillips investigated seven descrete exurban communities in the Kentucky Bluegrass to gain insights into their commuting behavior. The seven localities included in the study varied widely in their size, origin, location, social status level and morphology. Four communities were informal stringtown settlements and the other three were: an organized development, a nucleated settlement and an organized stringtown settlement.

The author used an interview schedule designed "to produce a general picture of the exurban commuter" on commuting journey, car pooling, perception of area, urban facilities and socioeconomic characteristics.[54] The survey revealed that the exurban areas sampled "were populated largely by young families with school age and pre-school age children."[55] The exurbanite households were most frequently headed by blue collar workers with relatively low education attainment and family income between $10,000 and $15,000 per year. The exurbanites chose their area of residence because of perceived advantages of open space, closeness to nature, friendly neighbors, peacefullness and safety.[56]

In the communities that Phillips surveyed the average commuting distances were about twenty miles, making exurbanites vulnerable to gasoline shortages and price fluctuations. With regard to car pooling,

23.3 percent of the main wage earners were car pooling and another 32.2 percent indicated that they would do so if they could find suitable pooling partners.[57]

The studies reviewed here show that the complex and culturally rich rural landscape of Kentucky's Inner Bluegrass region has many distinctive types of settlements. A new and important element in the settlement morphology of the Bluegrass is the exurban subdivision, which is described within the broader framework of rural settlement types.

Bluegrass Settlement Morphology

An examination of the General County Highway Maps[58] which show all roads, rural farm, nonfarm, and seasonal residences and commercial establishments revealed that there were essentially five types of rural settlements in the Bluegrass based on morphology and farm/non-farm characteristics. These were:

1. Linear farm - a pattern characteristic of farm houses paralleling a road (Figure 3A).

2. Linear non-farm with higher densities where rural non-farm lots face sections of highway (Figure 3B). Although reasons for the selection of such building lots may vary, in most cases the evidence indicated that original land owners had sold lots bordering the public highways, to realize a greater return from their capital investment than if the property had been left in agriculture.[59]

3. Radial nucleated settlements - may develop at road intersections (Figure 3C and D).

4. Unplanned nucleations - in the form of clustered settlements were developed prior to World War II in Kentucky. "Hamlets" and "villages" as defined by Rucker (reviewed earlier), and Negro hamlets, defined by

21

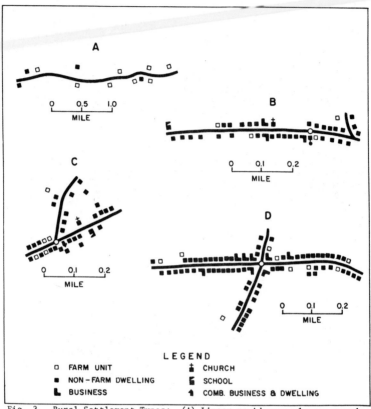

Fig. 3. Rural Settlement Types: (A) Linear residences along a rural route, north of Georgetown, Scott County, Kentucky; (B) Linear residences at higher densities, Finchville, Shelby County, Kentucky; (C) radial settlement formed at 'Y' intersection, Newtown, Scott County; and (D) radial settlement with dwellings at crossroads, Stringtown, Anderson County.

Smith, would be included in this category
if they meet their specifications (Fig. 4).

5. Exurbs - planned residential subdivisions,
    including mobile home parks (Fig. 5). These
    are differentiated from other settlement
    types by being promotional subdivisions, with
    an internal street pattern, which are of
    recent origin in that they have made their
    appearance in the Bluegrass since World
    War II.

The generalized settlement types are by no means
unique to the Bluegrass since an examination would
probably reveal the existence of most of these types
in other areas of Kentucky and regions of the United
States. Whereas the linear, radial and unplanned
nucleated residential pattern has been studied in
the Bluegrass context, theareal distribution of
exurbs has not yet been the subject of any comprehensive study. This study is designed to fill this
research gap.

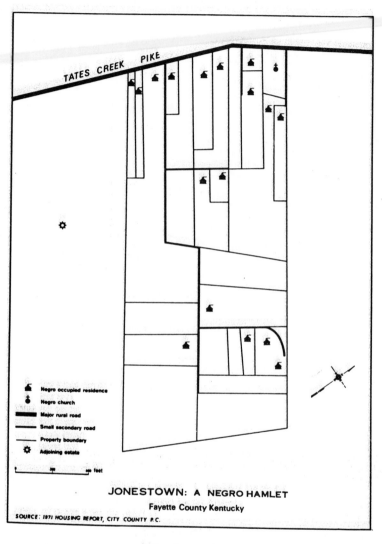

JONESTOWN: A NEGRO HAMLET

Fayette County Kentucky

SOURCE: 1871 HOUSING REPORT, CITY COUNTY P.C.

Fig. 4.

24

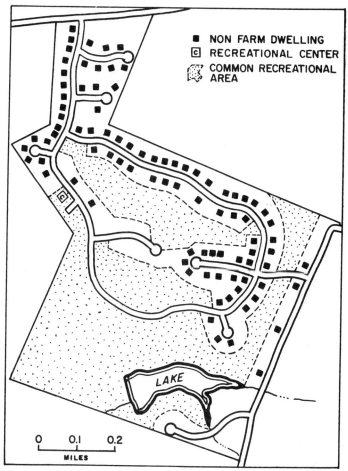

Legend:

■ NON FARM DWELLING
ⓒ RECREATIONAL CENTER
▨ COMMON RECREATIONAL AREA

LAKE

0   0.1   0.2
MILES

Source: Field reconnaissance by author

Fig. 5.   Greenbrier Estates in Fayette County Kentucky illustrates an exurb with residences located along a vermicular street pattern.

25

2. LAND CONVERSION AND THE RESIDENTIAL DEVELOPMENT PROCESS

The encroachment of cities on rural areas is of national concern. It is especially great in Kentucky's Bluegrass where exurban encroachment is highly visible on the horse farm landscape. John Fraser Hart notes that this concern is motivated by three more or less interrelated anxieties: (1) uncontrolled development is economically wasteful in the cost of land, construction and transportation or in the provision of such municipal service such as streets, schools, parks, utilities, water, sewers, fire, and police protection, garbage collection, snow plowing, and dog catching: (2) urban expansion is depriving the nation of some of its prime agricultural land; and (3) urban sprawl is an obvious abomination that does irreparable damage to some rather vague but fragile thing that is defined only as "the environment" or as "the ecology."[1]

This chapter will examine the process by which rural lands are converted to urban purposes. Insights into such a process are important in dealing with exurbs or planned residential developments which are located beyond the urban fringe.

The difficulty in obtaining estimates of growth in exurban territory is at once apparent because of the wide variety among such estimates that are available. After a careful review of a variety of sources, Hart found "such a wild array of estimates, ranging from 350 thousand to more than 5000 thousand acres a year," indicating "that some can be little more than sheer guesswork."[2] To overcome this difficulty Hart used two sets of data to obtain independent estimates of the amount of land which is being converted to urban uses in the United States. The first data set was on urbanized areas which are designated by the U.S. Bureau of the Census since 1950. Using this source Hart found that "the total amount of land in urbanized areas increased from 23,804.6 thousand acres in 1950 to 24,978.5 thousand acres in 1960 and 35,080.8 thousand acres in 1970."[3] This represented increases of 1,217.4 and 1,010.2 thousand acres per year from 1950-1970 respectively. The second data set consisted of "urban and built up" acreage for each county compiled in 1958 as part of the National Inventory of Soil and Water Conservation Needs (CNI). Using this source "the built up area of the United States in 1967 totalled 60,993 thousand acres and that it was increasing at a rate of 1,148 thousand acres a year."[4]

The CNI data for the Commonwealth of Kentucky showed that there were 836 thousand acres in urbanized and built-up areas in 1967 representing an increase of 14.2 percent over 1958 acreage.[5] Whereas most of this increase in urbanized land took place at the fringes of the existing urbanized areas, exurban residential developments also contributed to the change in urban acreage. Urban subdivisions are usually characterized by higher population densities than exurban developments that have relatively lower densities because of large lot zoning and mostly single family dwellings.

Residential Land Values

The price of a building lot represents the cost of the total conversion from farm to urban. The land conversion process is marked with an appreciation of residential lot values over farm land values. The farmer, upon the sale of his land for exurban development, makes an immediate gain on his investment whereas the developer must sell a given number of service lots to break even on his investment, thereafter additional lots sold result in profit.

The prices of serviced sites for single family residences, the components of these finished lot prices, the opportunity costs of the farm land used, and the development costs of layout, grading, sewering, and installation of improvements must be understood if the exurbia process is to be evaluated.

Schmid reviewed two studies, one on a San Francisco housing development and another on a Lisle, Illinois subdivision, for which data on improvement costs and changes in the size of lots was available.[6] The general lack of similar studies for other United States cities was acknowledged by Schmid who outlined the procedures for making such estimates as follows:

> Two important data items are required
> before the amount of appreciation contained
> in lot prices compared with production costs
> can be calculated. First, the number of
> lots per acre of raw land must be known so
> that the agricultural value of the raw
> land used for each lot can be calculated.
> Secondly, the average size of lot in major
> cities plus the cost of its improvement
> must be known. The dangers of the residual
> approach employed here should be noted.
> Errors in any of the components show up
> in the residuals and may distort them.
> Firm conclusions must await better data
> inputs.[7]

Schmid used the National Association of Home
Builders (NAHB) site value data and United States
Department of Agriculture (USDA) farm price to
compute the suburban raw land price appreciation
above farm land prices. His data for Kentucky
cities, reproduced in Table 3, show that there is
considerable variability in the appreciation of
farm land between cities of the state. Nationally,
the 1960 and 1964 total appreciation values were
399 percent and 1,875 percent in the total conversion
process.[8]

Lot Price Appreciation and Improvement Costs

Using NAHB data and assuming 2.6 lots per acre
(based on the Lisle, Illinois study), Schmid computed
the price per finished lot. Next the farm value of
the land in the lot was calculated and added to the
lot improvement costs and the total was subtracted
from the finished lot price to obtain the amount of
absolute appreciation. This appreciation was then
expressed as a percentage of the farm value. (See
Table 4). The 1964 NAHB data for 259 U.S. cities
"range from zero to 16,345 percent, with an average
of 1,875 percent." The fact that there is variation
in the lot price appreciation from city to city is
also apparent when cities within a state are examined.
(Table 4).

Schmid acknowledges the difficulty in quanti-
fication of the exact appreciation in the total

Table 3. Suburban Raw Land Prices Appreciation Above
Farm Land Prices, Kentucky Cities, 1964

City	Suburban price/acre	Farm price/acre	Appreciation (1)-(2)	Percent Appreciation over farm value (3)÷(2)
	(1)	(2)	(3)	(4)
Covington	$2,988	$171	$2,817	1,647%
Lexington[a]	3,300	171	3,129	1,830
Louisville	3,784	171	3,613	2,113
Owensboro	2,765	171	2,594	1,517
Paducah	11,500	171	11,329	6,625

a
An interview with Richard C. Sutherland revealed that in
1976 suburban raw land prices in Lexington range between
$5,000-$5,500 per acre, and farm prices range between
$1,800-$2,700 per acre. Sutherland is a land developer
with Blue Sky, Inc., Lexington, Kentucky.

Source: This table was abstracted from a larger table
containing data on U.S. cities in Appendix Table A-8 in
Allen Schmid Converting Land from Rural to Urban Uses,
Washington, D.C.; Resources of the Future, Inc., 1968. It
was based on Suburban raw land prices from National Association of Home Builders, Economic News Notes, Special Report
65-8 (Washington). Farm prices are state averages from
U.S. Department of Agriculture, Farm Real Estate Market
Developments, CD-66, pp. 13-14.

Table 4. Lot Price Appreciation Above Farm Land and Improvement Costs, 1964

City	Price per lot	Farm Value per lot	Farm Value plus improvement cost (2)+$2,435	Appreciation (1)-(3)	Percent Appreciation over costs (4)÷(3)=100	Percent Appreciation over farm value (4)÷(2)=100
	(1)	(2)	(3)	(4)	(5)	(6)
Covington	$3,766	$66	$2,501	$1,265	51%	1924%
Lexington	4,471	66	2,501	1,970	79	2996
Louisville	4,401	66	2,501	1,900	76	2889
Owensboro	3,121	66	2,501	620	25	943
Paducah	3,200	66	2,501	699	28	1063

Source: This table was abstracted from a larger table containing data on U.S. cities in Appendix Table A-3 in A. Allen Schmid Converting Land from Rural to Urban Uses, Washington, D.C.; Resources of the Future, Inc., 1968. It was based on suburban raw land prices from National Association of Home Builders, Economic News Notes, Special Report 65-8 (Washington). Farm value per lot was obtained by using a constant 26 lots per acre over the farm price/acre as shown in the preceding table.

conversion process and in obtaining a breakdown of
the appreciation to show how much is captured at
each stage in the conversion process due to the
unavailability or weakness of such data. However,
he does attempt to approximate the situation in
the conversion process, thus:

No claim is made that the tabulation
(See Table 5) is a valid statistical summary
However, it is the author's judgement that it
does not represent an extreme case. For an
acre of farmland valued at $300, the farmer
might receive about $1,332. The active
developer-builder might pay about $3,030,
and add $6,331 in improvement costs. If the
finished lots sold at about $10,072 per acre,
the appreciation would be $3,441 per acre.[9]

In another study on suburban land appreciation
Schmid observed that percentage change in poulation
growth of the central city and its urbanized area,
percentage change in land area, median family income
and percentage of population living on the fringes
are significantly associated with price appreciation.[10]

THE RESIDENTIAL DEVELOPMENT DECISION PROCESS

This section of the chapter will focus on the
nature of decisions, decision factors and decision
agents in the single family residential development
process. Edward J. Kaiser and Shirley K. Weiss at
the Department of City and Regional Planning of the
Unversity of North Carolina have guided several
extensive research projects related to residential
land development.[11] They have recently published
a study entitled "Decision Agent Models of the
Residential Development Process -- A review of
Recent Research."[12] upon which this section will
draw.

Kaiser and Weiss identified the decision of
the predevelopment landowner to sell or hold his
land, the decision of the residential developer to
locate subdivisions, and the decision of the household to move and to choose another location, in a

Table 5. Land Prices at Various Stages in the Conversion Process: A Composite*

	(Dollars per acre)
Farm land value[a]	300
Price farmers receive for subdivision use (1961)[b]	1,332
Price paid by developers for raw land (1964)[c]	3,030
Improvement cost ($2,435 x 2.6 lots/acre)[d]	6,331
Selling price of improved lots (1964) ($3,874 x 2.6 lots/acre)[e]	10,072
Total appreciation above farm land value (less improvement costs)	3,441
Percentage appreciation above farm land value[f]	1,147%

[a]A purposely high judgment of average U.S. farm land value weighted to those states with the most populous cities. The 1964 average value of farm land in the 48 states was $137.

[b]USDA data from Table 11. Simple average of regional averages without weighting.

[c]NAHB data from Appendix Table A-8.

[d]Data from Table 5.

[e]NAHB data from Appendix Table A-3.

[f]This composite produces a lower estimate of appreciation than the average shown in Appendix Table A-3 because of the higher farm land values used here.

*Source: This table has been reproduced from A. Allan Schmid, _Converting Land from Rural to Urban Uses_, Washington, D.C.: Resources for the Future, Inc., 1968. p. 26 All references in the footnotes of the table are to the original source.

33

conceptual model of the residential land development process (See Figure 6). Land use on the rural-urban fringe may be thought of as going through several stages in the process from nonurban to active residential use. Thus, the land could be considered as (1) acquiring interest for urban use; (2) being actively considered by an entrepreneur for purchase and development; (3) being programmed for actual development; (4) being developed; and finally (5) being purchased and inhabited by a household.[13]

The second row of Figure 6, lists the decision agents "each guided by his own incentives -- the household by basic needs and preferences, the developer-entrepreneur by the profit motive, the predevelopment landowner by a mixture of pecuniary and personal motives. The decisions...are the ones that land use controls must influence if local government is to affect the pattern of change."[14]

Decisions of the Predevelopment Landowner

The decision of a landowner to hold or sell the land depends on the qualitative aspects of farming such as the relative satisfaction the farmer derives from his way of life, and the quantitative aspects, such as the income received from the land which included the net annual holding cost of the land, costs that would be incurred in shifting to another investment, opportunity costs of capital and time period of investment.[15]

With regard to the analytical framework for the landowners Kaiser and Weiss write:

> Within the macroenvironment of contextual factors there are three main elements in modeling the landowner's tendency to hold or sell his property: (1) the characteristics describing the landowner that determine his reaction to pressure for sale; (2) property characteristics that affec not only its attractiveness to developers, consumers, and speculators and hence its market value for urban development, but also the ability of the land to supply monetary or psychic income to the landowner in its present use; and

34

	1 Urban interest	2 Active consideration for development	3 Programmed for development	4 Active development	5 Residence
Sequence of states					
Description of state	A decision agent considers the land as having development potential within a given time period	A decision agent has contacted another agent regarding the possible sale or purchase of the land	A decision agent has a definite idea of the timing and character of development	A decision agent has begun physical development of the land	A decision agent has purchased the residential package of house and lot
Sequence of key decisions	Decision to consider land		Decision to purchase land	Decision to develop land	Decision to purchase home
Decision agents					
Key:	Landowner Developer		Landowner Developor	Developer	Consumer
Supporting:	Realtors Financiers Public officials		Realtors Financiers Public officials	Realtors Financiers Public officials	Realtors Financiers Public Officials

Decision Process

Decision factors	Contextual characteristics		Decision agent characteristics		Property Characteristics
Local public policies			Policy guides and implementation instruments		

Figure 6. The residential land development process: sequence of states, key decisions, decision factors, and local public policies.

Source: Edward J. Kaiser and Shirley F. Weiss, "Decision Agent Models of the Residential Development Process - A Review of Recent Research", Traffic Quarterly, Vol. 23, No. 4, October 1969, p. 599.

(3) the form of the model itself which consists of the relationships of the landowner and property characteristics as inputs and the "sold" or "held" classification of lands as the output[16]

Kaiser and Weiss used the above conceptualization for an empirical analysis of the landowner behavior in Greensboro and Winston-Salem, North Carolina. Their research indicated that those most likely to sell their land to a developer are absentee owner, retired persons, joint owners of land and those who had their land either for less than ten years or for more than forty years.[17] While an empirical study of predevelopment landowners is not within the scope of this research, it is assumed that the exurban predevelopment landowner in the Bluegrass probably has some characteristics that are somewhat similar to those described by Kaiser and Weiss.

The Developer's Locational Decision

The housing developer is an entrepreneur who transforms raw land into residential units. If the developer feels that a tract may generally fill the specifications for the market he is seeking to meet, or that there exists a potential demand for housing appropriate to a specific site called to his attention, and if he can obtain a tentative agreement from the landowner to sell, he then proceeds to the next decision stage in his locational decision process-- the land purchase decision.[18]

The importance of the central role of the developer was the subject of an empirical study in Vancouver, British Columbia in which the author, Michael A. Goldberg, was interested in the supply of the housing market.[19] He used a questionnaire to solicit information on locational criteria, land acquisition, financing factors, contacts with public and private institutions and expectations of future development trends in housing types.

While Goldberg's research was particular to Vancouver, British Columbia, his results are generally applicable to residential development in North America. His findings were:

(1)   developers require property land in reasonable
       quantities before development will be con-
       sidered,

(2)   developers do not appear to be speculators in
       land,

(3)   developers interact with a number of local
       government agencies and citizen groups,

(4)   leverage is extremely important in financing
       residential developments, and banks, insurance
       companies, and federal funds are important
       adjuncts to retained earning and other private
       equity in providing sources of funds,

(5)   there appears to be a trend away from tradi-
       tional types of housing and tenure (i.e. single
       family, low rise and high rise) toward newer
       condominimum forms which make more efficient
       use of scarce urban land through higher average
       densities,

(60   increasing government intervention into resi-
       dential development process has resulted in
       longer lead times in planning projects.[20]

    McBridge and Clawson, after a review of three
case studies on land conversion concluded that the
process can best be described as one of negotiation.
Hence:

        The success or failure of those in the
    business depends on their ability to negotiate
    on a day-to-day basis. On the other hand, land
    use planners, citizens' association, conserva-
    tionists, proponents of outdoor recreation and
    open space, and other special interest groups
    are generally in the position of having to
    respond to crisis and to accomodate. The
    nature of the negotiation-accomodation pro-
    cess appears to be the root of the problem
    of monitoring and influencing land conversion.[21]

    Before proceeding to a discussion of the con-
sumers decisions in the residential development
process findings on the developers views on suburban

versus exurban land development and some observations about the exurban development process will be presented.

Developer's Views on Suburban Versus Exurban Land Development

In order to gain insights into why developers of residential land chose exurban sites over suburban sites several developers in the Bluegrass were interviewed.[22] Among the reasons given for exurban site development were: the need for housing in a rapidly growing area, the availability of developable land, the lower cost of raw land, the location of the land on a good highway, and less stringent subdivision regulations.

Table 6 is based on information obtained from three suburban and three exurban developers in the Bluegrass. Since information on the cost of raw land, improvements, and profits represent data of a highly sensitive nature it was not possible to obtain a large sample size. However, information on the six developers offer cases from which the following generalizations are formulated.

In general the cost of an acre of raw land in exurbia is one-third to one-half of that in suburbia. The mean value of raw land was $7,216 per acre in the suburban areas compared to a mean of $3,064 per acre in exurban areas. The improvements that a developer makes and the per acre cost of improvements vary from subdivision to subdivision. These costs are determined by such factors as the topography, the quality of streets and sidewalks, and the installation of utility lines that are borne by the developer and later included in the selling price of the improved lots. Improvements made by the suburban developers averaged $12,132 per acre compared to $6,244 per acre in exurban developments. This difference in improvement costs suggests that in some exurban areas developers provide only minimum subdivision standards. The mean profit margin for the suburban study areas was $3,785 per acre compared to $10,470 per acre in the exurban developments. The average lot size in exurban areas was larger in exurban areas compared to suburban areas as indicated lot sizes of 0.65 and 0.4 acres respectively. The comparison of the subdivisions indicates that exurban site development

TABLE 6

PROPORTIONATE BREAKDOWN OF DEVELOPERS COSTS[a]

	Suburb One		Suburb Two		Suburb Three	
	Amount (per acre)	Percen- tage	Amount (per acre)	Percen- tage	Amount (per acre)	Percen- tage
aw Land	$ 5,647	22	$ 7,000	35	$ 9,000	38
mprovements	$17,500	68	$ 8,000	40	$10,895	46
rofit	$ 2,567	10	$ 5,000	25	$ 3,789	16
otal	$25,667	100	$20,000	100	$23,684	100
average Lot ize (acre)	0.3		0.5		0.4	
ice of Impro- ed lot	$ 7,700		$10,000		$ 9,474	
umber of Lots	360		80		116	
creage in lots	108		40		46	

	Exurb One		Exurb Two		Exurb Three	
	Amount (per acre)	Percen- tage	Amount (per acre)	Percen- tage	Amount (per acre)	Percen- tage
aw Land	$ 3,333	25	$ 2,860	10	$ 3,000	15
mprovements	$ 6,667	50	$ 7.064	28	$ 5.000	25
rofit	$ 3,333	25	$16,076	62	$12,000	60
otal	$13,333	100	$26,000	100	$20,000	100
Average Lot ize (acre)	0.6		0.25		1.1	
rice of Impro- ed lot	$ 8,000		$ 6,500		$22,000	
umber of Lots	91		157		104	
creage in lots	54.6		39		114.4	

[a]Based on interviews with six developers in the Bluegrass area of Kentucky.

appeals to developers because of the lower costs of raw land, relatively few and less stringent improvement requirements and higher profit margin.

Development of Exurbs

Exurbs are a result of organized land subdivisions. The *Land Subdivision Regulations* of Fayette County, Kentucky defines subdivision as: the division of a parcel of land into two or more lots or parcels for the purpose, whether immediate or future, for sale, lease or building development, or if a new street is involved, any division of a parcel of land; providing that a division of land for agriculture purposes into lots or parcels of five acres or more and not involving a new street shall not be deemed a subdivision.[23]

The development of an exurb is a systematic step-by-step process which includes the acquisition of land for subdivision, preliminary and final approval of a land subdivision plat, by the local planning and zoning commission, the county engineer and utility company representatives. The approved plat is then recorded with the appropriate county clerk's office.

Small exurbs with up to twenty-five lots are usually developed as a single unit. However, in the larger subdivisions a parcel-by-parcel development process is followed. This is well illustrated in the case of Greenbrier Estates where, after the development of the first unit of 22 lots, approval was obtained at different times for a parcel-by-parcel development of 105 lots (See Table 7).

The Household's Decisions

The discussion in the preceding sections has been geared to the production side of the housing market. This section of the chapter will be devoted to an understanding of the residential change based on the consumer's decision process.

"The household's selection of a residence is actually the second of two related decisions in the residential mobility process. The first is the

TABLE 7

PARCEL-BY-PARCEL DEVELOPMENT OF LAND,
GREENBRIAR ESTATES, FAYETTE COUNTY, KENTUCKY

Unit/ Parcel Number	Plat Approval Date	Type of Approval	Number of Lots	Acreage	Street Length
1	June-1966	Preliminary	22	39.6	2,760 Ft.
1	September-1968	Final	22	39.6	2,760
2	June-1969	Preliminary	146	355.4*	16,170
2A	November-1970	Final	22	21.6	2,209
2B	November-1970	Final	14	13.9	1,192
2C	March-1972	Final	20	21.5	1,600
2D	July-1972	Final	20	26.2	2,172
2E	May-1973	Final	10	14.2	422
2F	August-1973	Final	4	5.7	1,918
2G	June-1973	Final	15	19.1	1,556

*Includes 151.7 Acre Golf Course

Source: Compiled by author from subdivision plats filed
at the Lexington Fayette County Planning Commission and
Property Valuation Office, Lexington, Kentucky.

decision to move...[and] the second decision, selection of a residence, provides the opportunity to link the residential mobility process with the land conversion process."[24]

The consumer stage of the residential development process is marked by more decision makers than those involved in earlier stages. Kaiser and Weiss have discussed the household's decision impact,

> ...in the aggregate this step determines the population that will reside in a particular sector of a community's space. By implication, it determines the relative success of the developer's locational decisions in terms of whether the subdivision development proceeds swiftly, slowly, or stalls. It determines, in part, the nature of the demand for urban services. Finally, it established linkages, particularly movement linkages, to other special, social and economic sectors of the community.[25]

Factors Influencing Decisions

Three types of decision factors clarify and explain the transition of property from a nonresidential state to residential development. These are contextual, decision agent, and property characteristics (See Figure 6), which influence the decision process of each decision agent. A possible configuration of decision agent models of the residential development process is illustrated in Figure 7.

Contextual factors include considerations that limit and determine the overall rate and type of change in the urban community and the general structure of decision agent and property characteristics.[26] Kaiser and Weiss also differentiate between socio-economic contextual factors which are suggested by the "economic structure and growth prospects of the urban area, community leadership, condition of local housing stock and market, local development industry concentration and competition, and the prevailing psychology of the period;" and public

42

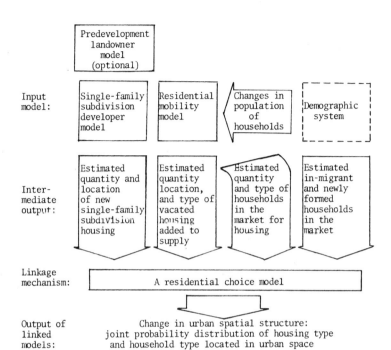

Input model:	Predevelopment landowner model (optional)			
	Single-family subdivision developer model	Residential mobility model	Changes in population of households	Demographic system
Intermediate output:	Estimated quantity and location of new single-family subdivision housing	Estimated quantity location, and type of vacated housing added to supply	Estimated quantity and type of households in the market for housing	Estimated in-migrant and newly formed households in the market

Linkage mechanism:

A residential choice model

Output of linked models:

Change in urban spatial structure: joint probability distribution of housing type and household type located in urban space

Figure 7. A linked model for the residential development decision process

Source: Edward J. Kaiser and Shirley F. Weiss "Decision Agent Models of the Residential Development Process-A Review of Recent Research", Traffic Quarterly, Vol. 23, No. 4, October 1969, p. 629.

policy contextual factors which include "annexation powers and the exercise of these powers; capital improvement, and services, policies affecting quality,.gross spatial pattern, and costs of transportatio, water, sewerage, and schools; and subdivision regulations, building codes, zoning, and land use plans."[27]

Property characteristics provide an operational means to describe the units of land (sites, parcels, zones, blocks, grid cells) about which decisions are made.[28] Kaiser and Weiss distinguish between three types of property characteristics: (a) physical characteristics, such as topography and soil conditions; (b) locational characteristics, which are derived from the relative location of the site, for example accessibility to employment areas and schools; and (c) institutional characteristics, such as the site's zoning category which is applied directly,to the site by social institutions.

Decision agent characteristics play an important role in determining the direction and the strength of the impact of contextual and property characteristics, and hence of public policy, on residential development.[29] The key decision agents in the residential development process are the landowner, the developer, and the consumer (Fig. 6).

Linked Decision Agent Model

In the final analysis of the residential development process Kaiser and Weiss brought together the three decision -- the predevelopment landowner, the developer and the household -- who were considered independently, into a linked model (See Figure 7). This model conceptualizes the simulation of site availability (landowner model); and brings together estimates of new houses (developer model) and vacated existing houses (mobility model); and links housing supply and demand (residential choice model).

Kaiser and Weiss acknowledge the difficulties in making the several linked models compatible. "The landowner model utilizes a sample of parcels, while the developer model uses geographic zones superimposed on the urban region and not coterminous with parcel boundaries. The developer model outputs locations, and an effort is underway to...include aminity price categories."[30]

In the summary to their extensive reivew of the residential development process Kaiser and Weiss suggest that future research efforts should be directed toward the improvement of their initial modeling effort and with the inclusion of "a predevelopment landowner model, a redevelopment model, a rental model, a housing decay model, and also a nonresidential development model, we would be moving closer to a total system of models for stimulating processes of spatial change in the urban environment."[31]

With increasing proportions of Americans living in suburbs and exurbs the process of converting rural land to residential subdivisions at the expanding suburban edge and beyond it in the exurban territory offers research possibilities to those interested in the land conversion process. The behavioral aspects of the predevelopment landowner, the developer, and the household; as well as the contextual, decision agent and property characteristics discussed in this chapter provide us with an understanding of the overall decision process.

In the Bluegrass area of Kentucky such factors as zoning stipulations, site topography, relative location, access to transportation routes and the perception of individuals and institutions involved in the exurban development process are important determinants of the spatial pattern of exurbs which makes its mark on the evolving landscape. These factors will be examined in chapter three, which will be devoted to a description of the pattern of exurban distribution.

45

3. THE DISTRIBUTION AND PHYSICAL QUALITY OF EXURBS

The following questions related to the distribution and nature of exurbs are discussed in this chapter.

(1) What is the areal distribution and extent of exurbs?

(2) Do exurbs vary in their physical quality? The empirical evidence gathered to analyze the first of the above questions will be utilized in developing a model of exurban location. The second question will be explored in the form of a hypothesis: exurbs vary in their physical quality (overall appearance of the exurb, including the type of dwellings and streets). An analysis of the quality of exurbs is also carried out as a basis for the selection of a sample to survey the socioeconomic characteristics and residential preferences of the exurbanites.

THE AREAL DISTRIBUTION OF EXURBS

As a preliminary step in pursuing the first of the two objectives outlined above, field reconnaissance of exurbs in the Bluegrass study area was carried out during June and July 1975. Exurbs were located on the basis of information provided by the local county government officials, including the county clerk, planners, property valuation officers, health inspectors, and real estate developers. The location of each exurb was plotted on General County Highway Maps.[1]

A total of one hundred exurbs were identified in the seven county study area (See Fig. 8 and Appendix I and II). Each exurb identified was surveyed and the number of dwellings in each was noted and a quality rating was assigned to each.[2]

The number of exurban residences in Kentucky's Bluegrass was found to be 4,146 of which 2,618, or 63.1 percent, are conventional dwellings and 1,528 or 36.9 percent, are mobile homes (See Table 8).

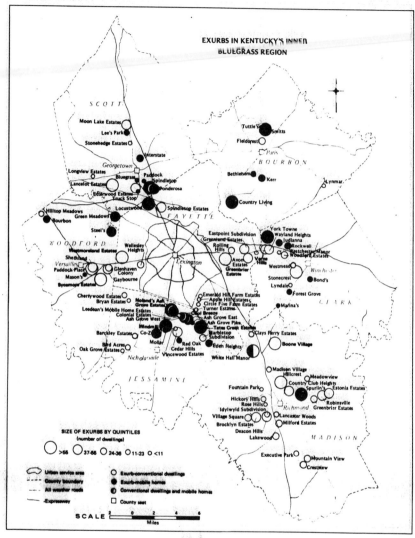

EXURBS IN KENTUCKY'S INNER BLUEGRASS REGION

SCOTT

Moon Lake Estates
Lee's Park
Stonehedge Estates
Interstate

Georgetown
Longview Estates
Lancelot Estates
Bluegrass   Paddock
            Spindletop
Elderwood Estates Ponderosa
Truck Stop
Hilltop Meadows   Locustwood
Green Meadows
Bourbon   Spindletop Estates
Steel's   FAYETTE

WOODFORD
Westmoreland Estates   Wellesley
Shetland   Heights
Versailles
Paddock Place   Glenhaven
Mason's   Colony
Sycamore Estates Gaybourne

Tuttle St.   Smitts
Fieldcrest

BOURBON
Bethlehem   Kerr
                           Lynmar
Country Living

Paris

Eastpoint Subdivision   York Towne
Greenland Estates   Wayland Heights
Rolling   Judianna
Hills   Rockwell
                    Westchester Manor
Avon   Woodford Estates
Estates   Valley
Greenbrier Hills
Estates   Westmead
Stonecrest   Bond's
Lyndale
Forest Grove

Winchester

CLARK

Cherrywood Estates
Bryan Estates
Noland's Ash
Grove Estates
Leedean's Mobile Home Estates
Colonial Estates
Ash Grove West
Barcksley Estates
Bird Acres   Co-Z
Oak Grove Estates Moller

Emerald Hill Farm Estates
Apple Hill Estates
Circle Five Farm Estates
Turner Estates
Capri Breeze
Ash Grove East
Ash Grove Pike
Tates Creek Estates
Marbletop
Subdivision
Minden II
Red Oak   Eden Heights
Cedar Hills
Vincewood Estates
White Hall Manor

Clays Ferry Estates
Boone Village

Marina's

Lexington

Nicholasville

JESSAMINE

Madison Village
Hillcrest   Meadowview
Country Club Heights Spurlin's   Estonia Estates
Fountain Park
Hickory Hills   Robinsville
Rose Hills   Greenbrier Estates
Idylwyld Subdivision
Village Square Richmond Lancaster Woods
Brooklyn Estates   Milford Estates
Deacon Hills
Lakewood   MADISON

Executive Park   Mountain View
                 Crestview

SIZE OF EXURBS BY QUINTILES
(number of dwellings)
○ >55   ○ 37-55   ○ 24-36   ○ 11-23   ○ <11

〰 Urban service area
--- County boundary
··· All weather roads
— Expressway
□ County seat

○ Exurb-conventional dwellings
● Exurb-mobile homes
◑ Conventional dwellings and mobile homes

SCALE 2 0 2 4 6
Miles

Fig. 8.

TABLE 8

THE DISTRIBUTION OF CONVENTIONAL DWELLINGS
AND MOBILE HOMES IN BLUEGRASS COUNTIES

County	Conventional Dwellings		Mobile Homes		Exurban Dwellings	
	Number	Percentage of Exurban Dwellings	Number	Percentage of Exurban Homes	Number	Percentage of Total
Bourbon	37	16.1	193	83.9	230	5.5
Clark	256	55.7	204	44.3	460	11.1
Fayette	384	80.5	93	19.5	477	11.5
Jessamine	159	23.7	513	76.3	672	16.2
Madison	976	88.5	127	11.5	1,103	26.6
Scott	204	38.6	324	61.4	528	12.7
Woodford	602	89.1	74	10.9	676	16.3
Total	2,618	63.1	1,523	36.9	4,146	100.0

Source: Survey by author.

49

There is considerable county to county variation in
the number of exurban residences. Whereas conventional dwellings make up the bulk of the residential
stock in Clark, Fayette, Madison and Woodford counties;
mobile homes exceed the number of conventional dwellings in Bourbon, Jessamine and Scott counties. A
total of 1,103 exurban dwellings, or over one-quarter
of the total, are in Madison county, the only county
in the study area without countywide planning. The
number of exurban dwellings in the other counties of
the Bluegrass study area ranges from a low of 230 in
Bourbon county to a high of 676 in Woodford County.

The mapped distribution of exurbs shows that
their existence is in part enhanced by the realtively
dense commuter highway network that is well established
in the Bluegrass (See Fig. 8). Access to all weather
roads is important to the automobile-bound exurbanites
who must make the daily journey to work. In a recent
survey of seven exurban communities in the Bluegrass,
Phillips found that the mean round-trip commuting
distances were 24.6 miles.[3]

To facilitate the interpretation of the spatial
distribution the one hundred exurbs of the Bluegrass
were grouped into quintiles on the basis of their
size (See Table 9). Over one-half or 53.3 percent of
the total exurban dwellings in the study area fell in
the first quintile. The percentage of dwellings in
the second, third, fourth, and fifth quintiles were
21.1, 14.2, 7.9, and 3.5 percent, respectively. The
average size of the exurbs, measured by the number
of dwellings for the one hundred exurbs in the study
area, was 41.5 dwellings. While Scott county's mean
size of 40.6 dwellings makes it typical to the all
exurban mean, three counties had higher and three
counties had lower mean exurban size. They were
Woodford--75.1, Bourbon--68.6, Madison--46.9; Fayette--
36.7, Clark--35.4, and Jessamine--32.0 dwellings per
exurb.

While exurbs are a discrete form of settlement
most exurbs in the Bluegrass are found in elongated
clusters aligned to the commuter road network. To
determine the extent to which there were groups
or clusters of exurbs a simple density based clus-
tering method was employed. A four square mile grid
was overlaid on a map showing the location of exurbs

TABLE 9

NUMBER OF DWELLINGS BY SIZE OF EXURBS

Size of Exurbs		Exurban Dwellings	
Quintile[1]	Range in Number of Dwellings	Number of Dwellings	Percentage of Total Exurban Dwellings
First	greater than 55	2211	53.3
Second	37-55	873	21.1
Third	24-36	588	14.2
Fourth	11-23	328	7.9
Fifth	less than 11	146	3.5
Total		4146	100.0

[1]Quintile of number of exurbs. There are 20 exurbs in each quintile.

per grid cell were used to make a density map (See Fig. 9). The following operational definition was used for the identification of a cluster. A cluster is a group of five or more contigious grid cells with a combined total of ten or more exurbs. A grid cell was considered contigious if it had one side or one corner lying adjacent to another cell containing an exurb. Using this ceiteria five exurban clusters were identified . Eighty-four percent of the exurbs lay within five clusters. Each of the five clusters was named after the city that was located closest to the cluster (See Fig. 9). The number of exurbs per cluster, in descending order were: Nicholasville--23, Richmond--21, Winchester--18, Georgetown--12, and Versailles--10. Of the 16 exurbs that were not in clusters Bourbon had 7 and Madison, Scott, and Woodford counties had 3 each.

While the exurbs surveyed are of recent origin, the earliest dating to 1958, it is possible to determine the areas where their development took place relatively early or recently. Subdivision plats for exurbs with conventional dwellings, filed at the county clerk's office in each of the study area counties, were used to obtain the date when a plat was officially recorded. This date usually marks the beginning of exurban development, although the actual improvements on the raw land, the construction of homes, and occupancy of completed homes begins at a later time. The data revealed a tri-modal distribution of exurbs with development at its peak in 1964, 1967 and 1972. The median date of exurban development was 1967. The development of exurbs started early, and at approximately the same time in the five exurban clusters identified previously. The data show that the earliest exurb developed in each cluster was: Richmond--1953, Winchester--1958, Versailles--1960, Georgetown--1963, and Nicholasville--1966. The first exurbs were followed by later development which took place in close proximity to the established exurbs. Fig. 10 shows the development of exurbs through five time periods. This temporal distribution of exurbs shows that each cluster had exurbs that developed during the earlier time periods, later exurbs were situated in close proximity to the existing exurban development.

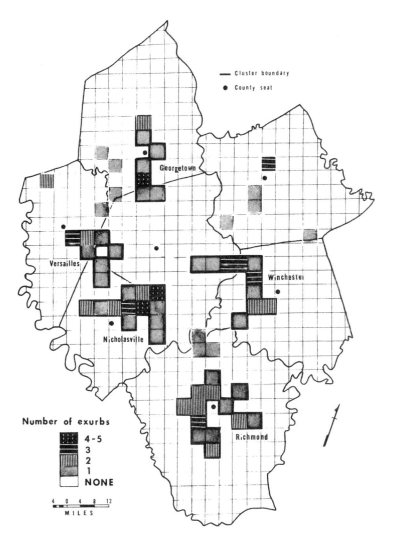

Legend:
Cluster boundary
County seat

Number of exurbs
4 - 5
3
2
1
NONE

4 0 4 8 12
MILES

Georgetown
Versailles
Nicholasville
Winchester
Richmond

Fig. 9. Density of Exurbs

53

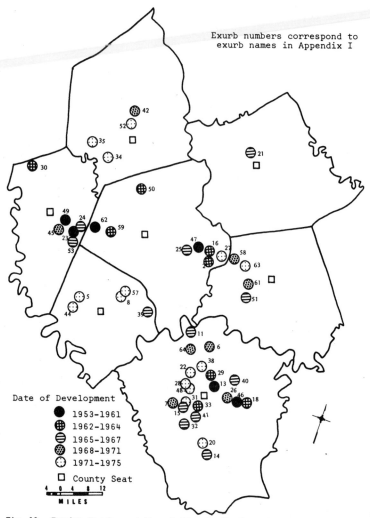

Fig. 10. Exurban Development Through Time for Exurbs with Conventional Homes

In summary it has been found that a healthy
housing market, the availability of cheap developp-
able land for subdivision, unrestrictive zoning[4]
and the existence of a good rural highway network
have contributed to the development of exurbs in
the Bluegrass.

EXURBAN POPULATION ESTIMATES

In this section estimates of the number and
proportion of exurban population for each of the
study area counties are made (See Table 10). The
following methodology is used to arrive at the
estimates. First, the number of rural non-farm
population and the number of dwellings are obtained
by using the 1970 United States census of the population. Secondly, the number of persons per dwelling
are computed by dividing the rural non-farm population by the number of rural non-farm dwellings.
The third step reqires taking the number of exurban
dwellings units and multipluing this figure by the
population per dwelling unit (as obtained in step
two). For comparative purposes the estimated exurban
population is then expressed as a percentage of the
rural non-farm population in 1970.

The above procedure is illustrated in the case
of Fayette county which had 9,993 rural non-farm
persons who were housed in 3,341 dwellings. Thus
the rural non-farm population divided by the number
of dwellings gives an average of 3.0 persons per dwelling. This figure is then used as a multiplier for
the exurban dwelling units. Thus Fayette county's
exurban population is estimated to be approximately
477 (the number of exurban dwellings) X 3.0, or 1,431.
A different multiplier is used in each county, to
give consideration to the variation in the household
population size. The exurban population estimates
arrived at by using the methodology above are given
in Table 8.

In the Bluegrass study area there are 12,438
exurbanites comprising an estimated 24.2 percent of
the rural non-farm population of 51,302 and 4.0 percent
of the total population of 309,429 in 1970. The total
exurban population in the study area is larger than
the mean population size of the county seats in

TABLE 10

RURAL NON-FARM AND EXURBAN POPULATION BY COUNTIES

County	Rural Non-Farm[a]			Exurban[b]		
	Dwelling Units Total	Population Number	Population Per Dwelling	Dwelling Unit Total	Population Number	Population Percentage of Total Rural Non-farm Population
Bourbon	2,163	5,984	2.8	230	644	10.8
Clark	2,071	6,310	3.0	460	1,380	21.9
Fayette	3,341	9,993	3.0	477	1,431	14.3
Jessamine	1,635	5,016	3.1	672	2,083	41.5
Madison	4,102	12,843	3.1	1,103	3,419	26.6
Scott	1,906	5,299	2.8	528	1,478	27.9
Woodford	2,025	5,857	2.9	676	1,960	33.5
Total	17,243	51,302	3.0	4,146	12,438	24.2

[a]Computed by the author using data from U.S. Bureau of the Census, Census of Housing: 1970, Vol. 1, Housing Characteristics for States, Cities and Counties, Part 19, Kentucky, Washington, D.C.: U.S. Government Printing Office, 1972, pp. 19-163 - 19-192.

[b]Survey by the author. Exurban population was computed by multiplying the exurban dwelling units by the respective counties population per dwelling.

56

counties adjacent to Fayette. Exurban population ranges from 644 in Bourbon county to 3,419 in Madison county. Because of the variation in the number of non-farm populations and the differing size of the counties it is more meaningful to compare the exurban developments' population as a proportion of the rural non-farm population. Thus expressed the figures range from a low of 10.8 percent in Bourbon county to a high of 41.5 percent in Jessamine county. The proportion of exurban population for Clark, Fayette, Madison, Scott, and Woodford are 21.9 percent, 14.3 percent, 26.6 percent, 27.9 percent and 33.5 percent, respectively.

LOCATION MODEL OF EXURBS

On the basis of the overall distribution of exurbs in the Bluegrass the following generalized location model of exurbs is presented. The model diagrammed in Figure 11 has four concentric zones which are described below.

Zone 1-represents the geographic city or the built up urban area whose fringes are marked by the other outer limits of the contigious suburbs. *Zone 2*-is mostly in non-urban land uses. The land adjacent to the built up urban fringe is under active urban growth consideration and held for speculation. The inflated land prices result in the development of urban exclaves or non-contiguous suburban subdivisions. Much of the second zone, however, is characterized by open land uses, such as forest, farm, or idle land. *Zone 3*-is where exurbs are located. An exurb is a discrete subdivision areally organized on an internal street pattern, located in a rural setting far enough beyond the frontier of suburban development so that it will not be engulfed by the expanding city in the foreseeable future. Exurban development is predicted on commuting. Exurbanites, for the most part, commute to work in nearby urban centers. A "commuter shed" or territory from which people commute to work can be identified for each major city. Phillips has identified the commuter shed for six metropolitan areas to which Kentuckians commute to work (See Fig. 12).[5] Seventy-eight of the 120 Kentucky counties have some commuting to a metropolitan

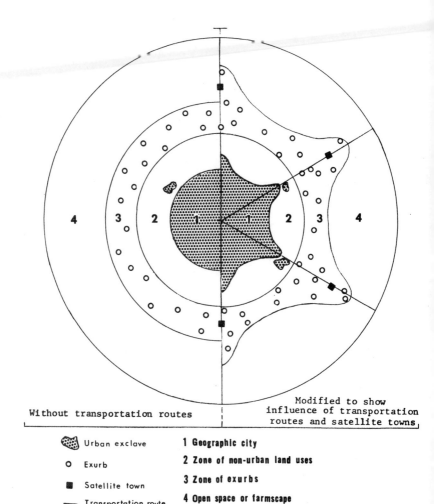

4	3	2	1	1	2	3	4

Without transportation routes

Modified to show influence of transportation routes and satellite towns

🌀 Urban exclave

○ Exurb

■ Satellite town

— Transportation route

1 Geographic city

2 Zone of non-urban land uses

3 Zone of exurbs

4 Open space or farmscape

Fig. 11.   Idealized locational model of exurbs.

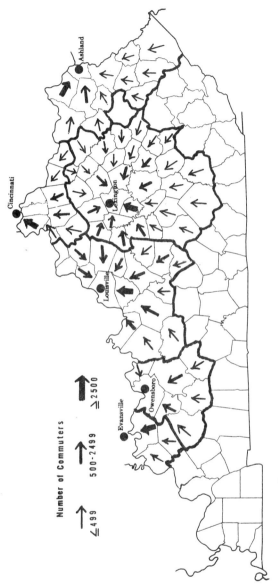

Figure 12. Kentucky's Metropolitan Commuter Sheds

Number of Commuters

≤499   500-2499   ≧2500

center and in some counties the commuter sheds over-
lap. Most of Kentucky's counties are "metropoli-
tanized", through commuting at least to some degree.[6]
Zone 4-is one of open space or rural farmscape in which
only a small percentage of the total population
lives.

The idealized exurban model assumes a rapidly
growing population and the availability of generally
flat to gently rolling land for the development of
exurbs in an economically ameniable environment. In
view of the strong influence of the transportation
routes one-half of the exurban location model is
modified to show the greater extent of development
along radial routes than in the interstices (Fig.11).
The density of exurbs also increases as one approaches satellite towns which lie in the shadow of
the primary urban centers. The satellite towns are
county seats with populations ranging between 5,000
and 17,000. While the primary urban centers provide
jobs, and high order goods and services to a large
proportion of exurbanites, industries in satellite
towns provide jobs for many additional exurbanites,
and satellite towns serve as convenient sources of
low order goods and services.

QUALITY RATING OF EXURBS

This section of the chapter is devoted to vali-
dating the hypothesis that exurbs vary in their physical quality. On the basis of field observation the
exurbs were quality-rated on a scale of one to six.[7]
The criteria used for rating are presented in Table
11, and the rating of each exurb is given in Appendix
I and II. In general the exurbs in Fayette county,
with somewhat more stringent subdivision development
policies since 1965, rate higher than the other counties in their overall quality. Fayette county's
landuse policies of containing urban growth within
the "urban service area"[8] (See Fig. 8) has created a
'doughnut' pattern with exurban growth taking place
just across the Fayette county boundary in the neigh-
boring counties where land prices, taxation, and rent
are lower and where subdivision development policies
are either at state minimums or have not been aggres-
sively supervised by local governmental officials.

60

TABLE 11

CRITERIA FOR QUALITATIVE RATING OF EXURBS

Rating*	Criteria
1.	Large, high value, custom built residences displaying considerable variation in architectural style. The dwellings are on large lots which are well landscaped. The exurb has a wide, high quality vermicular street pattern and paved sidewalks.
2.	Medium size and valued homes with some variation in architectural style, where owner probably selected from one of several alternative designs. Dwellings front on medium width curvilinear streets and have sidewalks which are usually paved.
3.	Basic two or three bedroom houses on small lots with little variation in the architectural style. Residences front on curvilinear and/or gridiron narrow streets, usually lacking in curbs and sidewalks.
4.a	Mobile home park in good overall appearance. All late model homes with manufactured skirting, situated on landscaped and well maintained lots. Paved high quality streets with sidewalks.
5.a	Mobile home park in fair overall appearance. All homes in fair condition with some some homes having skirting, and some lots landscaped. Paved hard surface streets without edging or curbs and sidewalks.
6.a	Mobile home park with poor overall appearance. Poorly arranged, mostly old homes in disrepair and without skirting, situated on unlandscaped lots. Unpaved or poorly maintained hard surface streets lacking in sidewalks.

aThe basic mobile home park requirements are specified by Kentucky Revised Statutes Chapter 219.310 to 219.410. The "good", "fair" or "poor" designation of mobile homes was derived from Thomas P. Field, Mobile Homes of Kentucky and the Lexington Hexagon: A Study in Areal Distribution. Kentucky Study Series #5, Lexington: Department of Geography and Fayette County Geographical Society, University of Kentucky, 1971.

*Residences in each rating category are shown in Figures 13-18.

61

Fig. 13.   Residence in a High Quality Exurb
with Conventional Dwellings

Fig. 14.   Residence in a Medium Quality Exurb
with Conventional Dwellings

62

Fig. 15.   Residence in a Low Quality Exurb
with Conventional Dwellings

Fig. 16.   Residence in a High Quality Exurb with Mobile Homes

Fig. 17. Residence in a Medium Quality Exurb with Mobile Homes

Fig. 18. Residence in a Low Quality Exurb with Mobile Homes

When mapped, the distribution of exurbs by quality shows that there is a complete range of exurbs within each of the five clusters (See Figures 19 and 10). Each cluster contains exurbs with conventional dwellings and mobile homes that are in the high, medium, and low quality categories. There were 4146 exurban dwellings in the study area which were distributed as follows: high quality conventional dwellings--12.4 percent; medium quality conventional dwellings--20.5 percent; low quality conventional dwellings--29.5 percent; high quality mobile homes--15.7 percent; medium quality mobile homes--17.5 percent; and low quality mobile homes--4.3 percent (Table 12). The distribution of exurbs shows that there is variation in the dwelling type and quality both within and between counties. For example Fayette county's 477 exurban residences were distributed as follows: high quality conventional dwellings--46.1 percent, medium quality conventional dwellings--34.1 percent, and high quality mobile homes--19.5 percent. The highest percentage values by quality rating in each county were: Bourbon county, low quality mobile homes--34.8 percent; Clark county, low quality conventional dwellings--48.5 percent; Fayette county, high quality conventional dwellings--46.1 percent; Jessamine county, medium quality mobile homes--50.6 percent; Madison county, low quality conventional dwellings--41.7 percent; Scott county, low quality conventional dwellings--35.8 percent; and Woodford county, medium quality conventional dwellings--52.8 percent.

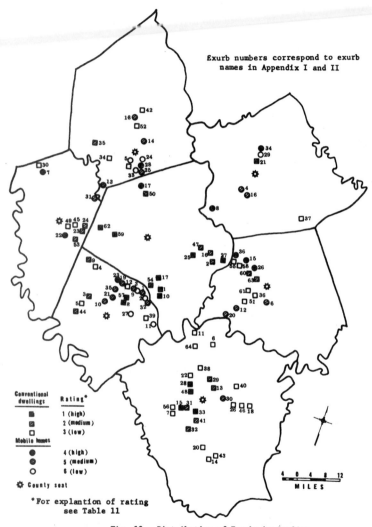

Fig. 19.   Distribution of Exurbs by Quality

TABLE 12

EXURBS AND EXURBAN DWELLINGS BY QUALITY RATING
FOR SEVEN BLUEGRASS COUNTIES

	QUALITY RATING G[1]						
	CONVENTIONAL DWELLINGS			MOBILE HOMES			TOTAL
	1(High)	2(Medium)	3(Low)	4(High)	5(Medium)	6(Low)	
COUNTY							
Bourbon							
Number of Exurbs	–	–	2	2	2	1	7
Number of Dwellings	–	–	37	75	38	80	230
Percentage of Exurban Dwellings in County	–	–	16.1	32.6	16.5	34.8	100.0
Clark							
Number of Exurbs	–	2	5	3	3	–	13
Number of Dwellings	–	33	223	161	43	–	460
Percentage of Exurban Dwellings in County	–	7.2	48.5	35.0	9.3	–	100.0
Fayette							
Number of Exurbs	8	4	–	1	–	–	13
Number of Dwellings	220	164	–	93	–	–	477
Percentage of Exurban Dwellings in County	46.1	34.4	–	19.5	–	–	100.0
Jessamine							
Number of Exurbs	2	3	4	1	8	3	21
Number of Dwellings	59	31	69	102	340	71	672
Percentage of Exurban Dwellings in County	8.8	4.6	10.3	15.2	50.6	10.6	100.0

TABLE 12--Continued

Madison							
Number of Exurbs	4	5	13.5	0.5	1	—	24
Number of Dwellings	237	250	460	29	127	1	1103
Percentage of Exurban Dwellings in County	21.5	22.7	41.7	2.6	11.5	—	100.0
Scott							
Number of Exurbs	—	1	4	1	4	3	13
Number of Dwellings	—	15	189	154	141	29	529
Percentage of Exurban Dwellings in County	—	2.8	35.8	29.2	26.7	5.5	100.0
Woodford							
Number of Exurbs	—	3	3	2	1	—	9
Number of Dwellings	—	357	245	36	38	—	676
Percentage of Exurban Dwellings in County	—	52.8	36.2	5.3	5.6	—	100.0
Study Area							
Number of Exurbs	14	18	31.5	10.5	19	7	100
Number of Dwellings	516	850	1223	650	727	180	4116
Percentage of Exurban Dwellings in the Study Area	12.4	20.5	29.5	15.7	17.5	4.3	100.0

[1]See Table 11.

68

SUMMARY

The two questions central to the chapter were:

(1) What is the areal distribution and extent of exurbs?

(2) Do exurbs vary in their physical quality?

To answer the first question, field reconnaissance was undertaken to locate the exurbs in the Bluegrass study area. A total of one hundred exurbs were identified and mapped. They contained 4,146 residences, of which 63 percent were conventional dwellings and 37 percent were mobile homes. The mapped distribution of exurbs was found to be closely oriented to the well established, relatively dense, highway network in the study area.

A simple density based method was used to identify exurban clusters. It was found that 84 percent of the exurbs fall within five clusters of 10 or more exurbs. The clusters were oriented to and elongated along transportation corridors.

It was estimated that there were 12,438 exurbanites in the Bluegrass study area as of July 1975. This total number constitutes approximately 24 percent of the rural non-farm and 4 percent of the total population, of 1970. The total exurban population estimate is somewhat larger in size than the mean population size of the satellite cities (Georgetown, Nicholasville, Paris, Richmond, Versailles and Winchester) in the study area.

The overall exurban distributional pattern was used as the basis of a locational model of exurbs. Four distinct zones were identified in the model. They were: zone one, the geographic city which extends to the edge of the contigious suburbs; zone two, comprising of nonurban land uses; zone three, in which exurbs are located; and zone four is open space and farm landscape. The exurban zone is located between a greenbelt of non-urban land uses and an extensive expanse of open space and farmland. One half of the exurban model was modified to show the greater extent of development along radial routes in the interstices.

69

The second area examined in this chapter was posed as a hypothesis--exurbs vary in their physical quality. A quality rating scale, which classified each exurb in one of six categories was developed and applied to each exurb. The classification was based on an overall rating which took into consideration such exurban attributes as the type, value and condition of housing; the quality of streets; and overall residential area appearance. A cross tabulation of the number of dwellings and exurbs for each county by exurban quality rating showed that there was variation in the physical quality of exurbs thus affirming the hypothesis that exurbs vary in their physical quality.

An examination of the location, size, and quality of exurbs described in this chapter was also undertaken with the view that these attributes will provide a basis for the selection of a sample to survey the socioeconomic characteristics and residential preferences of the exurbanites. The methodology and the results of the survey are discussed in the next chapter.

4. THE SOCIOECONOMIC CHARACTERISTICS AND RESIDENTIAL PREFERENCES OF THE EXURBANITES

The areal distribution of exurbs was examined in the preceding chapter and a qualitative rating of the exurbs was made. This rating is used in this chapter to design a sampling strategy to focus on the question--what are the socioeconomic characteristics and residential preferences of the exurbanites? In this study two hypotheses, one related to the socioeconomic characteristic of the exurbanites and the other related to the residential move of the exurbanites are proposed. These hypotheses are: (1) exurbanites will vary in their socioeconomic characteristics, and (2) most exurbanites will have moved to the exurbs from suburbia. The first hypothesis is based on the author's observation that, contrary to the commonly accepted image of exurbs as exclusive residential areas, exurban communities vary in their physical appearance and condition and thus should vary in their socioeconomic status levels.[1] The second hypothesis extends the suggestion by Sylvia F. Fava that many Americans are now moving beyond the suburbs to exurban communities.[2]

METHODOLOGY

The basic premise that guided the design of the sample survey was that there is variation in the socioeconomic characteristics of the exurbanites and that this variation is closely related to variations portrayed in the quality rating in Chapter three. Hence, communities selected were stratified to allow comparison on similar measurements between several exurban communities with varying characteristics.

A preliminary step in the selection of the sample for a survey of the exurbanites was the determination of the distribution of exurbs which was discussed in the preceding chapter. The exurban communities selected for the survey are shown in Fig. 8. and the sample size is given in Table 13. The criteria for selecting the exurbs are discussed below.

TABLE 13

SAMPLE SIZE FOR EXURBS SELECTED FOR STUDY

Exurb	County	Exurb Rating[1]	Number of Dwellings	Sample Size[2]	Actual Interviews
Boone Village	Madison	3	60	30	27
Cool Breeze	Jessamine	6	41	21	19
Greenbrier Estates	Fayette	1	89	45	42
Nolands Ash Grove Estates	Jessamine	4	102	26	27
Sycamore Estates	Woodford	2	287	72	71
Tates Creek Estates	Jessamine	5	102	26	19
Verna Hills	Scott	3	41	21	19
Westmoreland Estates	Fayette	1	82	41	45
Windmill	Jessamine	5	58	29	29
			862	311	298

[1]Each of the exurbs was rated on a scale of 1 through 6. The criteria for rating are outlined in Table 11.

[2]A fifty percent sample was used for exurbs with less than 100 dwellings and a twenty-five percent sample was used for exurbs with 100 dwellings or more.

72

A purposive sampling method was used because of the distributional analysis which enabled the selection of exurbs by quality and dwelling type. A judgmental sample also enabled to keep the sample size to a manageable number as well as reducing interviewer travel costs.

Two exurbs from Fayette county were selected because of the proportionally larger number of conventional dwellings of high quality in the county. The exurbs were Greenbrier Estates, which has large homes on large lots of one to two acres; and Westmoreland Estates, which has large homes on medium size lots of one-half to one acre. One exurb, Sycamore Estates, situated in Woodford county was included to represent the medium quality conventional dwellings which are found in it. One exurb each from Madison and Scott counties was selected to represent low quality conventional dwellings which comprise a larger proportion of the exurban dwellings in these counties. They were: Boone Village, Madison county, which is an established exurb; and Verna Hills, Scott county, which is a relatively new development.

Four exurbs in Jessamine county were selected for sampling exurbs with mobile homes because (1) a high proportion of the exurban residences in Jessamine county are mobile homes, and (2) Jessamine county has mobile homes in the low, medium, and high quality categories--representing the complete range of mobile home parks classified in this study. The exurbs selected in Jessamine county were: Noland Ash Grove Estates, a high quality park, Windmill, a medium quality park in which the residents pay a monthly lot rent; Tates Creek Estates, a medium quality exurb in which the residents own their lots; and Cool Breeze, a low quality exurb with mobile home parks.

To keep the sample size to a manageable number it was decided to use a fifty percent sample size in exurbs with less than 100 dwellings and a twenty-five percent sample size in exurbs with 100 dwellings or more. While no attempt was made to include conventional dwellings and mobile home parks in proportion to their numbers in the entire study area, the percentage of actual interviews is within 6.1

percent of their proportion in the study area (Table 14).

Exurbs selected for the sample survey represent the complete spectrum of exurbs both in their quality and dwelling type. Since each of the 100 exurbs in the Bluegrass was classified by quality and dwelling type, generalizations based on the survey may be extended to similar exurbs in the Bluegrass. It was hoped that the study would have wider application in other areas.

An interview schedule was designed to gather information on two broad categories:

A. Background Information: age, sex, marital status, place of work, occupation and income of each resident household member, etc.

B. Residential Preferences: Childhood and previous residence, duration and reasons for living in the present site, satisfaction with the developer and neighborhood, etc. (See interview schedule-- Appendix III).

SURVEY RESULTS

An analysis of the exurbanites responses to the interview questions was undertaken at two levels. First, the general population and socioeconomic characteristics of the exurbanites are discussed. Second, the residential preferences including the residential site selection process are analyzed.

I. SOCIOECONOMIC CHARACTERISTICS OF THE EXURBANITES

The Bluegrass exurban population surveyed indicated the median age of family heads is 37.3 years (Table 15). This median age is at a low of 28.5 years in Cool Breeze and is at a high of 49.1 years in Westmoreland estates and is typified by Sycamore's 37.2 years. In general, the median age of the head goes up with the quality rating of the exurb. The only exceptions to this general trend are Boone Village and Tates Creek Estates.

Table 14

COMPARISON OF DWELLING TYPES IN THE STUDY
AREA AND THE SAMPLE

	Study Area		Sample		Actual Interviews	
	Number	Percentage	Number	Percentage	Number	Percentage
Conventional Dwellings	2589	62.4	209	67.2	204	68.5
Mobile Homes	1557	37.6	102	32.8	94	31.5
Total	4146	100.0	311	100.0	298	100.0

TABLE 15

SELECTED EXURBAN POPULATION AND DWELLING CHARACTERISTICS

	Conventional Dwellings					Mobile Homes				All Exurban
	Greenbrier Estates	Westmoreland Estates	Sycamore Estates	Verna Hills	Boone Village	Nolands Ash Grove Estates	Tates Creek Estates	Windmill	Cool Breeze	
Quality Rating[1]	1(High)	1(High)	2(Medium)	3(Low)	3(Low)	4(High)	5(Medium)	5(Medium)	6(Low)	
A. Age of head (Median)	40.8	49.1	37.2	30.4	32.0	29.3	34.1	29.1	28.5	37.3
B. Age of wife (Median)	39.1	44.3	34.0	29.3	31.5	27.5	32.5	25.8	26.5	34.1
C. Travel time of head (mi., one way)	15.1	15.4	19.7	14.9	24.6	20.2	20.3	15.4	20.5	19.7
D. Travel time of wife (if wage earner)	15.1	15.5	19.9	19.8	29.8	20.3	19.8	25.0	25.0	20.0
E. Cars in family	2.1	2.1	2.0	1.9	2.0	1.9	1.8	1.7	1.2	2.0
F. Median value of owner occupied dwellings (dollars)	100,000	79,667	49,900	39,900	34,750	6,100	12,000	5,500	N.A	45,300
G. Price range of owner occupied dwellings (thousands of dollars)	60-250	60-125	40-58	32-50	28-50	4-14	11-18	2-10	N.A	2-250

[1]See Table 11.
Source: Survey by author.

76

For the discussion of the socioeconomic status (SES) of the exurbanites, three closely linked inicators: income, education, and occupation, were chosen.[3] Spearman's rank order correlation coefficients for these variables in the survey were: income and education, 0.50; income and occupation, 0.50; education and occupation 0.59. All these correlation coefficients were significant at the .001 level of significance (See Table 16). While income is usually good measure of social status , education and occupation add depth to this measure and give an inference regarding "life style", particularly if the age of the respondent is specified.

The wide range of family income distribution shown in Table 17 substantiates the notion that exurbs are not only the havens of the wealthy as implied by Spectorsky.[4] Individual exurbs range in their modal income from $5,000 to $7,999 in Cool Breeze to Greenbrier Estates where 45 percent of the households are in the $50,000 or more bracket. All exurban mobile home parks, with the exception of Cool Breeze have a modal income of $10,000 to $14,999. This is also the category within which lie thirty-eight percent of the families in Verna Hills, which has conventional dwellings. The modal categories for Boone Village and Sycamore estates and Westmoreland Estates are $15,000-$19,999, $20,000-$29,999 and $30,000-$34,000, respectively.

The mean number of wage earner for all exurban areas was 1.4 which is typified by Boone Village. The remainder of the exurban communities were divided equally between those that had higher and those that had lower number of wage earners than the all exurban mean. The number of persons depending on the family income also varied from a low of 2.4 persons in Noland Ash Gove Estates to a median of 3.5 persons in Boone Village to a high of 4.2 persons in Cool Breeze and Westmoreland Estates.

Educational levles for all exurban areas are generally higher than for the Lexington SMSA or Kentucky. 87.6 percent of the exurbanites in the Bluegrass had 4 years of high school or more, compared to 60.1 percent for the Lexington SMSA and 38.5

TABLE 16

CORRELATION COEFFICIENTS BETWEEN SELECTED
SOCIOECONOMIC STATUS VARIABLES FOR
ALL EXURBAN AREAS[1]

	Occupation	Education	Income
Occupation	1.00	0.59	0.50
Education		1.00	0.50
Income			1.00

[1]Spearman's Rank Order Correlation was used. All
correlation coefficients are significant at the 0.001
level of significance.

TABLE 17

FAMILY INCOME OF EXURBANITES
(percentage distribution)

	Conventional Dwellings						Mobile Homes			
Family Income, 1975	Greenbrier Estates	Westmoreland Estates	Sycamore Estates	Verna Hills	Boone Village	Nolands Ash Grove Estates	Tates Creek Estates	Windmill	Cool Breeze	All Exurban
	N=38	N=38	N=55	N=16	N=24	N=25	N=19	N=29	N=17	N=261
Quality Rating[1]	1(High)	1(High)	2(Medium)	3(Low)	3(Low)	4(High)	5(Medium)	5(Medium)	6(Low)	
Under $2,999	-	-	-	-	-	8.0	5.3	10.3	5.9	2.7
$3,000-4,999	-	-	1.8	-	-	8.0	5.3	3.4	17.6	3.1
5,000-7,499	-	2.6	-	-	4.2	8.0	-	3.4	29.4	3.8
7,500-9,999	-	-	1.8	-	4.2	8.0	10.5	20.7	17.6	5.7
10,000-14,999	-	2.6	7.3	37.5	20.8	32.0	42.1	34.5	11.8	16.7
15,000-19,999	7.9	2.6	12.7	31.3	29.8	20.0	10.5	17.2	17.6	14.6
20,000-24,999	7.9	18.4	29.1	31.3	25.0	8.0	10.5	10.3	-	16.7
25,000-29,999	-	7.9	29.1	-	8.3	8.0	5.3	-	-	9.2
30,000-34,999	10.5	21.1	12.3	-	4.2	-	10.5	-	-	8.4
35,000-39,999	10.5	15.8	3.6	-	-	-	-	-	-	4.6
40,000-44,999	5.3	5.3	1.8	-	4.2	-	-	-	-	2.3
45,000-49,999	13.2	7.9	-	-	-	-	-	-	-	3.1
Over $50,000	44.7	15.8	-	-	-	-	-	-	-	8.8
Mean number of wage earners	1.3	1.8	1.5	1.3	1.4	1.6	1.5	1.3	1.2	1.4
Mean number of persons depending on family income	4.2	3.6	3.7	3.3	3.5	2.4	3.4	2.6	4.2	3.5

[1]See Table 11.
Source: Survey by author.

79

percent for the state in 1970.[5] The percentage of exurbanites who were college graduates ranged from zero in Cool Breeze to 65.9 percent in Westmoreland Estates. The modal education levels for Boone Village, Sycamore Estates and Greenbrier Estates were high school graduate, some college, and Bachelors Degree, respectively (Table 18).

Occupation of the main wage earner is an important SES characteristic. Table 19 shows the proportion of exurbanites in each exurb who are in different occupational categories. The first nine categories are based after the U.S. Census,[6] which gives a general rank from highest (professional) to lowest (service). Four additional categories: retired, unemployed, disabled and homemaker, were added to cover the households where the head of household did not work.

Over half the labor force in Cool Breeze, Nolands Ash Grove Estates, Tates Creek Estates and Windmill was employed in "blue collar" occupations (craftsmen, operatives, laborers, farm workers or service workers).

Boone Village and Verna Hills had a lower proportion of professional and managerial workers but a higher proportin of clerical, craftsmen, and operatives than in Sycamore Estates Greenbrier Estates and Westmoreland Estates. This finding is not surprising in view of the fact that the latter areas had a higher quallity rating and housing value than the former areas.

Earlier statements by Clawson[7] on the characteristics of the exurbanites suggested that a large number of retired persons reside in exurban areas. This study revealed that there were no retirees in four exurbs and the proportion of such persons varied from 2.1 percent in Westmoreland Estates to 16.7 percent in Nolands Ash Groves Estates. The higher proportion of retirees in mobile home developments indicates that mobile homes offer cheap housing for retired persons and others who are on fixed incomes.

To measure the degree of variation in the exurbs, a simple measure, the Coefficient of Relative Variation (CRV), was used[8] (Table 20) In comparing two or more areas, higher CRV values indicate more variation, conversely low CRV values imply less

TABLE 18

EDUCATION LEVEL OF PRINCIPLE WAGE EARNER

Level of Education	Conventional Dwellings						Mobile Homes			All Exurban
	Greenbrier Estates	Westmoreland Estates	Sycamore Estates	Verna Hills	Boore Village	Nolands Ash Grove Estates	Tates Creek Estates	Windmill	Cool Breeze	
	N=42	N=44	N=70	N=19	N=26	N=25	N=18	N=28	N=19	N=291
Quality Rating[1]	1(High)	1(High)	2(Medium)	3(Low)	3(Low)	4(High)	5(Medium)	5(Medium)	6(Low)	
1st-8th grade	2.4	-	1.4	5.3	5.8	8.0	22.2	17.9	36.8	7.2
Some high school	-	2.3	1.4	26.3	3.8	-	11.1	7.1	36.8	5.2
High school graduate	4.2	9.1	15.7	26.3	25.9	48.0	38.9	32.1	21.1	21.0
Some college	35.7	22.7	37.1	31.3	23.1	24.0	11.1	28.6	5.3	27.1
Bachelor's Degree	40.5	22.7	32.9	10.5	23.1	8.0	16.7	14.3	-	24.4
Some graduate school	2.4	6.8	-	-	7.7	4.0	-	-	-	3.1
Masters Degree	9.5	15.9	8.6	-	3.8	4.0	-	-	-	6.5
Doctoral or Professional	4.8	20.5	2.9	-	7.7	4.0	-	-	-	5.5

[1]See Table 11.

Source: Survey by author.

TABLE 19

OCCUPATION OF MAIN WAGE EARNER

	Conventional Dwellings						Mobile Homes			All Exurban
Occupational Category[1]	Greenbrier Estates	Westmoreland Estates	Sycamore Estates	Verna Hills	Boone Village	Nolands Ash Grove Estates	Tates Creek Estates	Windmill	Cool Breeze	
Quality Rating[2]	N=42 1(High)	N=45 1(High)	N=69 2(Medium)	N=17 3(Low)	N=27 3(Low)	N=24 4(High)	N=18 5(Medium)	N=28 5(Medium)	N=18 6(Low)	N=290
Professional	35.7	55.6	43.5	26.3	33.3	16.7	27.8	14.3	-	33.4
Managerial	54.8	33.3	40.6	21.1	29.6	8.3	-	14.3	5.6	29.3
Sales	9.5	6.7	5.8	-	14.8	4.2	5.6	10.7	-	6.9
Clerical	-	2/2	-	10.5	7.4	12.5	5.6	-	-	3.1
Craftsmen	-	-	2.9	15.8	11.1	16.7	11.1	14.3	11.1	6.9
Operative	-	-	-	5.3	3.7	4.2	33.3	25.0	11.1	6.2
Laborers	-	-	-	-	-	12.5	11.1	3.6	11.1	2.8
Farm	-	-	-	-	-	-	-	-	11.1	0.7
Service	-	-	1.4	10.5	-	4.2	-	7.1	33.3	4.1
Retired	-	2.2	5.8	-	-	16.7	-	7.1	5.6	1.7
Unemployed	-	-	-	10.5	-	-	5.6	3.6	5.6	.7
Disabled	-	-	-	-	-	-	-	-	5.6	0.3
Homemaker	-	-	-	-	-	4.2	-	-	-	0.3

[1] Based on 1970 Census of Population, Classification Index of Industries and Occupation, Washington, D.C., U.S. Government Printing Office, 1971.

[2] See Table 11.

Source: Survey by author.

82

TABLE 20

COEFFICIENTS OF RELATIVE VARIATION (CRV) FOR SELECTED SOCIOECONOMIC STATUS VARIABLES[1]

(percentage distribution)

	Conventional Dwellings					Mobile Homes				
	Greenbrier Estates	Westmoreland Estates	Sycamore Estates	Verna Hills	Bcone Village	Nolands Ash Grove Estates	Tates Creek Estates	Windmill	Cool Breeze	All Exurban
Quality Rating[2]	1(High)	1(High)	2(Medium)	3(Low)	3(Low)	4(High)	5(Medium)	5(Medium)	6(Low)	
Occupation	6.8	15.7	28.9	47.8	47.6	57.4	41.3	48.1	65.1	36.5
Education	27.7	35.8	31.8	26.9	44.5	52.4	54.3	46.2	46.8	43.8
Income	22.0	26.4	25.4	14.4	33.9	40.3	37.6	36.6	44.4	43.3

[1]The Coefficient of Relative Variation is computed by dividing the standard deviation by the mean and multiplying the product by 100.

[2]See Table 11.

variation. The CRV's for all sample areas combined
were: occupation--36.5 percent, education--43.8
percent, and income 43.3 percent. In general the
CRV's for exurbs with mobile homes were higher than
for exurbs with conventional dwellings. Also the
higher quality exurbs tended to have a lower CRV's
than medium and low quality exurbs. Due to the
absolute price constraint in the high quality exurbs
residents in such areas tend to have lower CRV's.
Conversely in low quality exurbs with conventional
dwellings and exurbs with mobile homes, where residence is based on choice rather than economic constraint, in general tend to have persons from a
wider cross section of socioeconomic status levels,
as reflected in the higher CRV values.

II. RESIDENTIAL PREFERENCES OF EXURBANITES

A number of studies have suggested that exurbanites prefer their residence because of perceived advantages of open space, closeness to nature,
friendly neighbors, peacefulness and safety.[9] Sylvia
Fava has suggested that exurbanites have moved from
the suburban areas rather than from the city.[10] This
research will attempt to provide empirical evidence
on the exurbanite's move to the exurbs, their site
selection process and residential preferences.

The results of 298 interviews in 9 exurban communities on their "reasons for living in this subdivision" are summarized in Table 21. The mean
ranking of interviewee responses on a scale of 1
(not important) to 3 (very important) for ten items
discussed below affirms the residential preferences
of the exurbanites.

The cost of housing, taxes, and being close to
work had the lowest overall rating in comparison
with other items that were rated. The low rating on
the item 'close to work' is reflected by the fact
that most exurbanites lived within twenty miles or
30 minutes of their work place. Exurban residents
considered peaceful, quiet surroundings very important as indicated by an overall rating of 2.8 on
a scale of 1 to 3. Open space and being close to
nature increased in importance with the qualitative
rating of the exurbs since higher quality implied

84

TABLE 21

EXURBANITES RESPONSES TO SELECTED ITEMS ON "REASONS FOR LIVING IN THIS SUBDIVISION"

Mean Ranking on Scale 1 (Not Important) to 3 (Very Important)

Item	Conventional Dwellings					Mobile Homes				All Exurban
	Greenbrier Estates	Westmoreland Estates	Sycamore Estates	Verna Hills	Boore Village	Nolands Ash Grove Estates	Tates Creek Estates	Windmill	Cool Breeze	
Quality Rating[1]	1(High)	1(High)	2(Medium)	3(Low)	3(Low)	4(High)	5(Medium)	5(Medium)	6(Low)	
Peaceful, quiet surroundings	3.0	2.9	2.8	2.5	2.6	2.8	2.8	2.8	2.4	2.8
Safe, low crime area	2.6	2.5	2.7	2.6	2.7	2.7	2.5	2.9	2.4	2.7
Open Space	2.8	2.9	2.7	2.1	2.5	2.4	2.8	2.7	2.4	2.6
Close to nature	2.4	2.7	2.3	1.9	2.2	2.4	2.7	2.6	2.5	2.4
Cost of housing	1.7	1.8	2.4	2.7	2.7	2.6	2.4	2.5	2.6	2.3
Low taxes	1.9	1.8	2.5	2.6	2.5	2.6	2.1	2.5	1.8	2.3
Friendly neighbors	2.0	2.1	2.3	2.3	2.5	2.5	1.6	2.6	2.5	2.3
Good Schools	2.1	2.1	2.1	2.2	2.4	1.7	1.8	2.0	2.1	2.1
Close to Work	1.9	1.6	1.8	2.4	1.9	2.1	1.5	2.3	2.1	1.9

[1]See Table 11.

Source: Survey by author.

85

larger lots and spacious living.

An analysis of the residential move history (Table 22) indicated that exurbs appeal to persons now living in an urban area, but brought up in rural or small town environments. The data show that 36.8 percent of the husbands were raised in rural areas and another 24.0 percent were raised in small towns. These figures dropped to 6.9 percent and 16.3 percent when exurbanites were asked about their immediate previous residence. This finding is consistent with the overall rural to urban movement of earlier times and it is also consistent with Sylvia F. Fava's observation that the residential moves of most Americans at the present time will be from suburb to suburb or suburb to exurb, as discussed in part below[11]. Indeed the move to exurban areas may in many cases, be directly related to a desire to recreate an earlier childhood living experience, made pleasant by the passage of time and the addition of urban amenities.

The hypothesis to be affirmed is that more exurbanites have moved to their present residence from suburban areas than from urban, rural or other exurban areas. When exurbanites in the Bluegrass were asked about their immediate previous residence, approximately four out of every ten exurbanites or 39.1 percent of the husbands and 38.6 percent of the wives indicated that they lived in suburbia before moving to the exurbs. The previous residence of the remainder of the exurbanites was: rural farm--7 percent, exurbs (countryside subdivisions)--16 percent, small town--16 percent, and city--22 percent. Although there is some variation from exurb to exurb in the percentage of exurbanites who have suburban backgrounds their proportions support the general hypothesis about the residential move to the exurbs mostly from the suburbs and to a lesser extent from the cities and rural areas.

To gain insights into the exurban residential search behavior, exurbanites were asked how they discovered their residence. The responses were: from driving around--42 percent, through a friend--23 percent, through a realtor--14 percent, from an advertisement (newspaper, radio, television)--13 percent, and other--8 percent (See Table 23).[12] These reasons vary from exurb to exurb. For

86

TABLE 22

RESIDENTIAL MOVE HISTORY

	Conventional Dwellings					Mobile Homes				
	Greenbrier Estates	Westmoreland Estates	Sycamore Estates	Verna Hills	Bocne Village	Nolands Ash Grove Estates	Tates Creek Estates	Windmill	Cool Breeze	All Exurban
Quality Rating[1]	1(High)	1(High)	2(Medium)	3(Low)	3(Low)	4(High)	5(Medium)	5(Medium)	3(Low)	
A. Median years of residence in present home	2.5	3.9	3.8	1.8	3.7	2.8	2.2	2.1	1.1	2.6
B. Husband's childhood residence (percentage distribution)										
1. a rural farm house	52.5	17.8	32.9	15.8	55.6	36.0	35.3	44.4	56.3	36.8
2. a countryside subdivision	2.5	8.9	11.4	-	7.4	-	5.9	-	-	5.6
3. a small town[1]	-	33.3	28.6	42.8	14.8	24.0	17.6	22.2	31.3	24.0
4. a city suburb	22.5	8.9	7.1	15.8	3.7	24.0	23.5	14.8	-	12.5
5. a city	22.5	31.1	20.0	26.3	8.5	16.0	17.6	18.5	12.5	21.2
C. Wive's childhood residence (percentage distribution)										
1. a rural farm house	40.0	18.2	20.9	21.1	42.3	24.0	37.5	44.4	31.6	29.1
2. a countryside subdivision	5.0	4.5	7.5	-	7.7	4.0	18.8	-	-	5.3
3. a small town	-	27.3	28.4	26.3	19.2	24.0	18.8	33.3	42.1	24.2
4. a city suburb	27.5	9.1	7.5	31.6	-	28.0	12.5	11.1	5.3	13.7
5. a city	27.5	40.9	35.8	21.7	30.9	20.0	12.5	11.1	21.1	27.7

TABLE 22 --continued

	Greenbrier Estates	Westmoreland Estates	Sycamore Estates	Verna Hills	Boone Village	Nolands Ash Grove Estates	Tates Creek Estates	Windmill	Coal Breeze	All Exurban
D. Husband's immediate previous residence (percentage distribution)										
1. a rural farm house	7.1	2.2	5.7	-	18.5	4.0	17.6	11.1	-	6.9
2. a countryside subdivision	16.7	13.3	12.9	15.8	22.2	8.0	11.8	14.8	41.▪	15.6
3. a small town	-	11.1	17.1	21.1	48.1	4.0	11.8	18.5	17.▪	16.3
4. a city suburb	61.9	53.3	40.1	36.8	-	43.0	41.2	25.9	17.▪	39.1
5. a city	14.3	20.0	24.3	26.3	11.1	36.0	17.6	29.6	23.▪	22.1
E. Wive's immediate previous residence (percentage distribution)										
house	7.1	2.3	5.9	-	15.4	8.0	18.8	11.1	5.3	7.4
2. a countryside subdivision	16.7	13.6	11.8	16.7	23.1	4.0	12.5	14.8	31.6	15.1
3. a small town	-	11.4	16.2	22.2	50.0	4.0	12.5	18.5	21.1	15.8
4. a city suburb	59.5	52.3	41.2	38.9	-	44.0	37.5	25.9	15.8	38.6
5. a city	16.7	20.5	25.0	22.2	11.5	40.0	18.5	29.6	26.3	23.2

[1]This category was added after interviewing in Greenbrier was completed. Thus for Greenbrier those indicating that they were from a small town were included in the 'city' category.

Source: Survey by author.

TABLE 23

EXURBANITES PERCEPTION AND BEHAVIOR ON SELECTED RESIDENTIAL QUESTIONS

	Conventional Dwellings					Mobile Homes				
Quality Rating[1]	Greenbrier Estates 1(High)	Westmoreland Estates 1(High)	Sycamore Estates 2(Medium)	Verna Hills 3(Low)	Boone Village 3(Low)	Nolands Ash Grove Estates 4(High)	Tates Creek Estates 5(Medium)	Windmill 5(Medium)	Cool Breeze 6(Low)	All Exurban
Preference for Subdivision Size										
1. Smaller	-	4.5	13.2	11.1	8.0	-	14.3	6.9	38.9	9.2
2. Same	92.7	90.9	86.8	72.2	92.0	96.2	78.6	93.1	27.8	85.2
3. Larger	7.3	4.5	-	16.7	-	3.8	7.1	-	33.3	5.7
Present Lot Size										
1. Too big	4.8	8.9	4.3	-	-	-	-	7.1	-	3.8
2. About right	88.1	91.1	72.5	89.5	80.8	96.3	68.4	78.6	27.8	79.2
3. Too small	7.1	-	23.2	10.5	19.2	3.7	31.6	14.3	72.2	17.1
Satisfaction with Developer										
1. Yes	55.0	100.0	77.1	72.2	33.3	92.6	42.1	96.6	42.1	72.1
2. No	45.0	-	22.9	27.8	66.7	7.4	57.9	3.4	57.9	27.9
Neighborhood Preference										
1. New	69.0	91.9	68.6	61.1	63.0	66.7	84.2	62.1	36.8	69.3
2. About same	21.4	2.2	17.1	27.8	18.5	25.9	10.5	17.2	15.8	16.6
3. Old	9.5	6.7	14.3	11.1	18.5	7.4	5.3	20.7	47.4	14.2
Knowledge about Present Residence										
1. thru a friend	26.2	15.6	27.1	15.8	11.1	33.3	21.1	31.0	15.8	22.9
2. thru a realtor	19.0	13.3	25.7	-	22.2	-	-	6.9	5.3	13.8
3. From driving	42.0	68.9	25.7	52.6	55.6	40.7	15.8	55.2	15.8	42.1
4. From an ad	-	2.2	8.6	31.6	7.4	14.8	47.4	3.4	52.6	13.1
5. Other	11.9	-	12.9	-	3.7	11.1	15.8	3.4	10.5	8.1

[1]See Table 11.
Source: Survey by author.

89

example, the proportionate number of those acquiring knowledge through a friend was high in Nolands Ash Grove Estates (33 percent), Windmill (31 percent), Sycamore Estates (27 percent), and Greenbrier Estates (26 percent). Realtors played relatively active role in the residential search of exurbanites in Sycamore Estates, Boon Village, and Greenbrier Estates where 26 percent, 22 percent and 19 percent of the respective exurb's residents obtained their home through a realtor. The majority of the exurbanites discovered their present home or lot through evening and weekend homehunting trips. The exurbs and proportion of their residents who acquired knowledge about their home or homesite through driving around were: Westmoreland Estates--69 percent, Boone Village--55 percent, Verna Hills--53 percent, Greenbrier Estates--42 percent, Nolands Ash Grove Estates--41 percent, Sycamore Estates--26 percent Cool Breeze--17 percent, and Tates Creek Estates--16 percent. Visibility of some of the exurbs from arterial highways seems to have been an important factor in attracting potential residents. Advertisement through the newspaper, radio and television also, played an important role in the residential search of the exurbanites. Thus the four exurbs in which the proportion of their population which exceeded the all exurban mean of 13 percent were: Cool Breeze--53 percent, Tates Creek Estates--47 percent, Verna Hills--32 percent and Nolands Ash Grove Estates--15 percent.

The exurbanite's preference on neighborhood size, lot size, satisfaction with the subdivision developer and neighborhood preference are shown in Table 23. The exurbs surveyed and their sizes, measured by the number of dwellings, were Cool Breeze and Verna Hills 41, Windmill 58, Boone Village 60, Westmoreland 82, Greenbrier Estates 89, Tates Creek Estates and Nolands Ash Grove Estates 102, and Sycamore Estates 287, dwellings. Exurbanites preferences for subdivision size varied with the type of problems the exurbanites were having. For example, with 41 mobile home units Cool Breeze tied for the smallest exurb surveyed. Yet 39 percent of its residents wished it were smaller, and another 33 percent of its residents wished it were larger, while 28 percent wished it would remain the same size. This difference in opinion is in part accounted for by the fact that Cool Breeze has problems of unpaved streets, sewer and storm water drainage which some residents believe would not be critical if the subdivision size were smaller, while others believe that with additional homes the problems mentioned would be solved. In Verna Hills, which also has 41 dwelling units, 72 percent of the residents wished the subdivision remain the same in size, 17 percent wished that it be larger and 11 percent wished that it be smaller.

Most of the exurbanites (79 percent) were satisfied with their lot size. Seventeen percent indicated that their lot size was too small and 4 percent felt their lots were too large. The average lot size in exurbs with mobile home parks were: Cool Breeze, 0.1 acre; Nolands Ash Grove Estates, 0.14 acre; Tates Creek Estates, 0.2 acre; and Windmill, 0.13 acre. The average lot size in exurbs with conventional dwellings were: Boone Village, 0.2 acre; Greenbrier Estates, 1.1 acre; Sycamore Estates, 0.4 acre; Verna Hills, 0.21 acre; and Westmoreland Estates, 0.92 acre. In Cool Breeze, a low quality rated mobile home park where the lots average one-tenth of an acre, 28 percent of the residents were satisfied with their lot size and 72 percent felt that their lots were too small. On the other hand Nolands Ash Grove Estates, an exurb with high quality rating, where mobile homes are located on average lot sites of 0.14 acre, 96 percent of the residents were satisfied with their lot size and only 4 percent felt that their lots were too small. In Boone Village, a low quality rated exurb with conventional dwellings on lots averaging 0.2 acre, four-fifths (81 percent) of the residents were satisfied with their lot size, and one-fifth (19 percent) felt their lots were too small. In contrast, Greenbrier Estates a high quality exurb with conventional dwellings and lots averaging 1.1 acre, the percentage of residents who felt their lots were about right, too small and too large were 88 percent, 7 percent and 5 percent, respectively.

When asked about their neighborhood preference 86 percent of the exurbanites reported that they liked their new neighborhood as well or better than their old neighborhood. Fourteen percent indicated their preference for their old neighborhood. Almost half (47.4 percent) of the residents in Cool Breeze indicated a preference for their old neighborhood compared to less than one-tenth (9.5 percent) of the residents in Greenbrier Estates who preferred their old neighborhood, indicating that the level of resident satisfaction varies with individual expectation of the quality of the exurb.

While the American ideal for living in a single family conventional dwelling and continued upward residential mobility seems to have been functional for most exurbanites, some exurban residents, especially those living in mobile homes, may be going through a period of downward mobility in their residential cycle.

Satisfaction with the developer varied with the quality of the exurbs and the problems the exurbanites were concenred about at the time of the survey. For example over one-half (58 percent) of the residents of Cool Breeze, a low quality rated exurb, were not satisfied with the developer because of unpaved streets, exposed sewage, and poor arrangement and spacing of homes which were among the problems cited by the resident. In contrast, almost half the residents in Greenbrier Estates, a high quality rated exurb, the single complaint of the residents was over the overflow of some of the septic tanks in the subdivision. Tates Creek residents cited storm water drainage and narrow streets without sidewalks as problems. Only in one exurb, Westmoreland Estates, which is a high quality rated exurb, the residents were unanimous in their satisfaction with the developer.

SUMMARY

A survey of selected exurban communities was - taken to determine the socio-economic status (SES) characteristics and residential preferences of the exurbanites. An examination of the income, education, and occupational levles of the exurbanites revealed that--contrary to the commonly perpetuated myth of the exclusive exurb--individual exurbs vary in their SES characteristics. For example, the

modal family income amount varied from the $5,000-
$7,999 bracket in Cool Breeze to the $50,000 or more
bracket in Greenbrier Estates. When asked about
their residential preferences, exurbanites as a
group preferred living in their countryside subdivision because of open space-close to nature environment; and peaceful, quiet, and safe surroundings.
Being close to work was relatively less important
to the exurbanites, whose trip to work averaged 19.7
miles. Individual exurbs varied in their overall
response to various items they were asked to rate
as 'a reason for living in this subdivision'. For
example, the item 'cost of housing', was relatively
unimportant to the residents in Greenbrier Estates,
moderately important to residents in Sycamore Estates, and very important to residents in Boone
Village. Questions related to the residential
move history of the exurbanites provided data to
substantiate the hypothesis that most exurbanites
have made their residential move from suburbs to
exurbs. Thirty-nine percent of the exurbanites
surveyed indicated that their previous residence
was in the suburbs. The remainer of the exurbanites had previously lived in rural farm (7 percent), countryside subdivision (16 perdent), small
town (16 percent), or city (22 percent).

5. SUMMARY AND OUTLOOK

In recent years many Americans have opted to live beyond the suburbs in islands of exurban development. These exurbs are the product of imaginative developers capitalizing on the latent desire of the consuming public for a rural way of life by offering them an alternative residential environment. The distinctive exurban settlement pattern that is evolving beyond the traditional geographic city was the subject of this research.

For the purpose of this study the term *exurb* was defined as a discrete, areally organized subdivision with an internal street pattern, located in a rural setting. It is an urban island in a rural setting, located far enough beyond the frontier of suburban development to preclude being engulfed by the expanding city within the forseeable future, yet it is within commuting range of a city. In this study, the residents were considered *exurbanites* regardless of their length of tenure in an exurb.

Three broad themes--the process of exurban development, the pattern of exurban distribution and the socioeconomic characteristics and residential preferences of the exurbanites were explored to gain insights into the exurban phenomenon that has been superimposed on the stable, culturally rich and picturesque landscape of the Kentucky Bluegrass.

The process of conversion of rural land to residential subdivisions involves the decision of the predevelopment landowner to sell or to hold his land, the decision of the residential developer to locate in an exurb in preference to a suburb, and the decision of the household to move to an exurb in preference to another residential setting. The decision process of each decision agent in the residential development of land is influenced by contextual, decision agent, and property characteristics.

The decision process that results in a developed exurb involves the complex linkage of opportunity, motivation and means. If the product of

95

this process is profit to all, the original vendor, the developer, and the residents, it is successful. A successful exurb, however, is not necessarily an unqualified benefit to the local community. A number of questions are appropriate; Is an exurb the best use of a particular parcel of land? Was there an urgent need for residences in this location? Is the exurb's contribution to its community equal to the built-in land costs of its eccentric location? The fact of a hundred exurbs in the study area suggest that these questions were either answered positively or not considered to be relevant at the time the initial decisions were implemented.

The development of an exurb is a systematic step-by-step process which includes the acquisition of land for subdivision, and preliminary and final approval of a land subdivision plat by the local planning and zoning commission, the county engineer, and utility company representatives. The approved plat is then recorded with the appropriate county clerk's office. Small exurbs are usually developed as a single unit. In the larger subdivisions a parcel-by-parcel development process is followed.

The following questions related to the distribution and nature of exurbs were posed:

(1) What is the areal distribution and extent of exurbs?

(2) Do exurbs vary in their physical quality?

(3) What are the socioeconomic characteristics and residential preferences of the exurbanites?

To answer the first question, field reconnaissance was undertaken to locate the exurbs in the Bluegrass study area. The result was a map of the areal distribution of exurbs. A total of one hundred exurbs were identified. They contained 4,146 residences, of which 63 percent were conventional dwellings and 37 percent were mobile homes. The mapped distribution of exurbs was found to be closely oriented to the well established, relatively dense, highway network in the study area.

96

A simple exurban density based method was used to identify exurban clusters. It was found that 84 percent of the exurbs fall within five clusters. The clusters were elongated in the direction of the transportation corridors.

It was estimated that there were 12,438 exurbanites in the seven Bluegrass county study area as of July 1975. This total number constitutes approximately 24 percent of the rural non-farm and 4 percent of the total population, of 1970. The total exurban population estimate is somewhat larger than the mean population size of the six county seats-- Georgrtown, Nicholasville, Paris, Richmond, Versailles, and Winchester--of the counties adjacent to Fayette county in the study area.

The overall exurban distributional pattern was used as the basis of a locational model of exurbs. For distinct zones were identified in the model. They were: zone one, the geographic city, which extends to the edge of the contiguous suburbs; zone two, the suburban frontier comprising of non-urban land uses and urban exclaves; zone three, in which exurbs are located lies beyond the frontier of urban development in the forseeable future but within the range of commuting from the city; and zone four, an area of open space and farmscape beyond the commuting range of the exurbanite. The exurban model was modified to show the influence of the smaller urban centers and the radial transportation routes.

The second question examined in this study was posed as a hypothesis--exurbs vary in their physical quality. A quality rating scale, which classified each exurb in one of six categories was developed and applied to each exurb. The classification was based on an overall rating which took into consideration such exurban attributes as the type, value and condition of housing; the quality of streets; and overall residential area appearance. A cross tabulation of the number of dwellings and exurbs for each county by exurban quality rating showed that there was variation in the physical quality of exurbs by county.

A survey of selected exurban communities was undertaken to determine the socioeconomic status (SES) characteristics and residential preferences of the exurbanites. An examination of the income, education, and occupational levels of the exurbanites revealed that--contrary to the original perception conceived in the context of a developing megalopolis of the exclusive exurb--individual exurbs vary in their predominent SES characteristics. For example, the modal family income amount varied from the $5,000-$7,999 bracket in Cool Breeze to the $50,000 or more bracket in Greenbrier Estates.. When asked about their residential preferences exurbanites as a group preferred living in their country-side subdivision because of open space-close to nature environment; and peaceful, quiet and safe surroundings. Being close to work was relatively less important to the exurbanites, whose trip to work averaged 19.7 miles. Individual exurbs varied in their overall response to various items they were asked to rate as "a reason for living in this subdivision." For example, the item "cost of housing", was relatively unimportant to the residents in Greenbrier Estates, moderately important to residents in Sycamore Estates, and very importnat to residents in Boone Village. Questions related to the residential move history of the exurbanites provided data to substantiate the hypothesis that most exurbanites have made their residential move from suburbs to exurbs. Thirty-nine percent of the exurbanites surveyed indicated that their previous residence was in the suburbs. The remainder of the exurbanites had previously lived in rural farm (7 percent), countryside subdivision (16 percent). small town (16 percent), or city (22 percent).

OUTLOOK

Some conjectures on the exurban phenomena and suggestions for monitoring its growth along with recommendations for further research are discussed below.

Over three centuries of settlement and population expansion have appreciably changed the American landscape. Cities and roads have been built and expanded at the expense of forest and agriculture land. As cities have become crowded there is spillover of people to urbanized corridors, nearby towns and subdivisions. While rising human population may account for the disappearance of open land, this loss may also be attributed to the level of technology. For example, the automobile not only permits people to live in housing developments much further from jobs and shopping facilities, it also permits people to visit areas that were once considered remote. The automobile and improved roads have greatly extended the commuting radius of Americans to the extent that exurbia has become the common state of the American countryside. As a commuter the exurbanite is part of the Daily Urban System of the United States, within which live more than 90 percent of the national population (See Fig. 20).[1] As commuters exurbanites put on more miles on their automobiles and spend more time on the highway than urbanites. For example, the round trip to work of exurbanites in this study was 40 miles compared to 14 miles for urban dwellers.[2]

The increasing cost of gasoline, motor vehicles and single family homes compared to personal income may act as deterrents to the continued expansion of exurban living. Also tighter land use controls at various governmental levels would go a long way toward establishing standards to eliminate such problems as might exist. Multi-county agencies such as the Bluegrass Area Development District should be given the tasks of identifying the problem areas and coordinate federal, state, and local efforts in the recognition and improvement of the social, economic, and physical conditions in the region.

Bluegrass Area Development District

The seven Bluegrass county study area lies at the core of a larger seventeen county area of the Bluegrass Area Development District BGADD, (See Fig, 21), which is recognized by national and state government agencies as the official regional planning organization.[3] Some of the problems identified by the BGADD are summarized in Table 24. The problem areas in the core counties were: water supply deficiencies in Bourbon, Clark, Fayette,and Scott counties; divergent land use policies in Fayette,

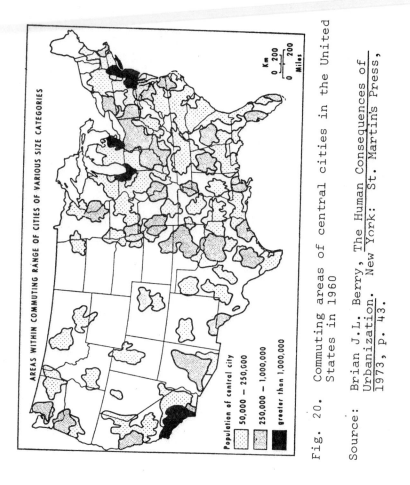

Fig. 20. Commuting areas of central cities in the United
          States in 1960

Source: Brian J.L. Berry, The Human Consequences of
         Urbanization. New York: St. Martin's Press,
         1973, p. 43.

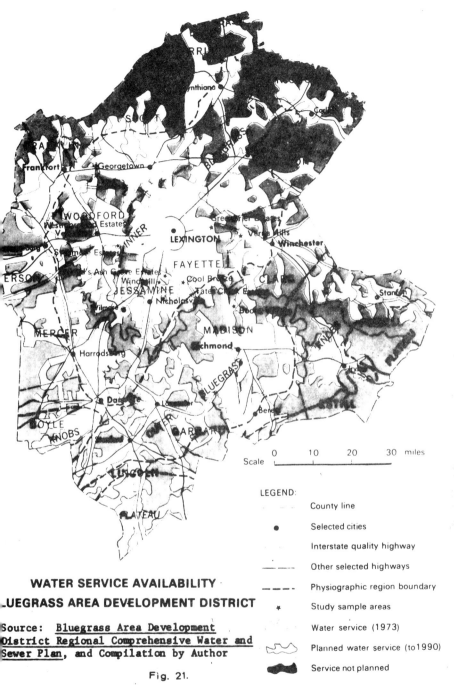

WATER SERVICE AVAILABILITY
BLUEGRASS AREA DEVELOPMENT DISTRICT

Source: <u>Bluegrass Area Development</u>
<u>District Regional Comprehensive Water and</u>
<u>Sewer Plan</u>, and Compilation by Author

Fig. 21.

Scale: 0   10   20   30   miles

LEGEND:

County line

● Selected cities

Interstate quality highway

Other selected highways

Physiographic region boundary

* Study sample areas

Water service (1973)

Planned water service (to 1990)

Service not planned

101

TABLE 24

PROBLEM AREAS IN THE
BLUEGRASS AREA DEVELOPMENT DISTRICT (BGADD)

Bourbon	Water supply problems, deficient highway links to Lexington
Clark	Water supply problems
Fayette	Water supply problems, divergent landuse policies
Jassamine	Divergent landuse policies
Madison	Divergent landuse policies
Scott	Water supply problems, divergent landuse policies
Woodford	None identified

Source: Summarized by author from Bluegrass Area Development District Preliminary Land Use Plan, 1972.

Jessamine, Madison, and Scott counties and; deficient highway links to Lexington in Bourbon county. Additional problems in the peripheral counties were related to housing deficiencies, and lack of access to arterial highways and intercity linkages.

Earlier in this study a close relationship between exurbs and transportation routes was indicated. A closer look at the pattern of exurban development reveals its orientation along water service lines. Fig. 21 shows how water lines have been extended along main highways producing a spider-web like pattern of water service through surprisingly large areas of the Bluegrass.[4] The extension of rural water service to cover a larger portion of the BGADD counites in the immediate planning period (defined as the next five years) and for long range planning period (defined as five to twenty year period) is shown in Fig. 21.

The availability of water and other urban services are important considerations in monitoring the growth of exurban development. For example, the minimum lot size requirements, of 10 acres in Fayette county and 5 acres in each of the counties adjacent to Fayette, for the construction of a single family dwelling with a septic tank act as a deterrent to the development of exurbs with small lots. While planned neighborhoods offer residential sites to those who opt for exurban living such development must be undertaken using cost benefit studies. Site development costs for proposed subdivisions usually omit many or most of the costs of development listed below:

(1) the cost of constructing and maintaining adequate road systems between the population center and the subdivision;

(2) the cost of transporting children to and from schools;

(3) the cost of constructing electric, telephone, and gas, utilities into outlying areas;

103

(4)   the cost of extending to the outlying areas a public water system and, in particular, a system sized to be capable of providing flows sufficient for fire fighting purposes;

(5)   the higher cost of fire insurance;

(6)   the cost of either conveying collected sewage long distances for municipal treatment or adopting interim measures for sewage disposal until a connection to a central treatment facility can be accomplished;

(7)   the cost of providing personnel and equipment necessary for adequate police and fire protection;

(8)   the cost of either providing additional parks and recreation opportunities in outlying areas or the additional cost of transportation and inconvenience of utilizing existing parks which are distant from the remote development;

(9)   the cost of constructing adequate storm drainage facilities which would be consistent with the long term needs of the area; and

(10) the added cost of rural mail delivery.[5]

The above list suggests some of the variables which may be incorporated in modeling and evaluating the proposals for subdivision development. Review of rural subdivision proposals by regional agencies would be one way of eliminating problems such as poor roads, inadequate drainage and sewers which occur in some exurban communities.

In concluding the study it is suggested that empirical investigation of the areal distribution and extent of exurbs be carried out in other areas of the United States and the results compared with the locational model of exurbs developed in this study. Also the three hypotheses used in this study should be applied to other localities. The hypotheses were: (1) Exurbs vary in their physical quality, (2) Exurbanites will vary in their socio-economic characteristics and, (3) Most exurbanites will have moved to the exurbs from suburbia.

FOOTNOTES

Chapter 1

[1]See Wilford A. Bladen "Evolution of a Compage: The Case of Lexington, Kentucky," Research Paper presented at the Annual Meeting of the Kentucky Academy of Science, Richmond, Kentucky; and Derwent Whittlesey, "The Regional Concept and the Regional Method," in Preston E. James and Clarence F. Jones, eds., American Geography: Inventory and Prospect, Syracuse, N.Y: Syracuse University Press, 1954, pp. 21-68. Whittlesey defined a compage as a region that approaches totality in its unity of physical, biotic and societal context.

[2]For a discussion on the temporal spread of cities in the U.S., see John R. Borchert, "American Metropolitan Evolution," Geographical Review, Vol. 57, 1967, pp. 301-323, and "Evolution of the Urban Pattern," Chapter 2, in Maurice H. Yeates and Barry J. Garner, The North American City, New York: Harper and Row, Publishers, 1976, pp. 22-50, Second Edition.

[3]U.S. Bureau of the Census, Census of Population, 1970, Detailed Characteristics, Final Report PC (1)-D1 United States Summary, Washington, D.C.: U.S. Government Printing Office, 1973.

[4]U.S. Bureau of the Census, Census of Population, 1970, Vol. 1. Characteristics of the Population, Part A., Number of Inhabitants, Washington, D.C.: U.S. Government Printing Office, 1973.

[5]Sylvia F. Fava, "Beyond Suburbia," The Annals of the American Academy of Political and Social Science, 422, November 1975, p. 10.

[6]John S. Adams, "Directional Bias in Intra-Urban Migration," Economic Geography, Vol. 45, 1969, pp. 302-323.

[7]For a discussion of urban density profiles see: Bruce Newling, "The Spatial Variation of Urban Population Densities," Geographical Review, Vol. 59, No.2, April 1969, pp. 242-252, Colin Clark "Urban Population Densities" Journal of the Royal Statistical Society, Vol. 114, Part 4, 1951. pp. 490-495; John S. Adams, "Residential Structure of Midwestern Cities" Annals of the Association of American Geographers, Vol. 60, No. 1, March 1970, pp. 37-62.

[8]James W. Hughes, "Dilemmas of Suburbanization and Growth Controls," The Annals of the American Academy of Political and Social Science, 422, November, 1975, p.63.

[9]Adams, op. cit., p.322.

[10]Phillips D. Phillips, Exurban Commuters in the Kentucky Bluegrass Region, Lexington: Center for Real Estate and Land Use Analysis, Monograph #5, 1976, p.1.

[11]Hughes, op. cit., p. 64.

[12]Brian J. L. Berry, "Population Growth in the Daily Urban System of the United States, 1980-2000," in the U.S., Commission on Population Growth and the American Future, Population, Distribution and Policy, p. 240.

[13]Richard Egan, quoting from an interview with Calvin L. Beale, "How Ya Gonna Keep 'Em in Metropolis After They've Seen the Countryside?" The National Observer, May 31, 1975, p. 3. Mr. Beale is an Agricultural Department demographer.

[14]Phillips, op. cit., p. 2.

[15]Environmental Protetion Agency, Control of Erosion and Sediment Deposition from Construction of Highways and Land Development, Washington, D.C., 1971, as cited in Gunnar Isberg "Controlling Growth in the Urban Fringe" Current Municipal Problems, Vol. 16, 1974-75, pp.87.

[16]John Fraser Hart, "Urban Encroachment on Rural Land" The Geographical Review, Vol. 66, No. 1, January 1976, p. 16.

[17]Karl B. Raitz, "The Bluegrass" in P.P. Karan (Editor) Kentucky: A Regional Geography, Dubuque, Iowa. Kendall/Hunt Publishing Company, 1973, pp. 53-72.

[18]Auguste C. Spectorsky, The Exurbanites, Philadelphia: J. P. Lippincott Co., 1955.

[19]Ibid, p. 6.

[20]Ibid, p.4.

[21]Webster's New World Dictionary, Second College Edition, New York: The World Publishing Company, 1972, p. 489.

[22]Maurice H. Yeates and Barry J. Garner, op. cit., p. 185.

[23]Ibid, p. 185.

[24] Ibid, p. 185.

[25] James E. Vance, Jr., "California and the Search for the Ideal," Annals of the Association of American Geographers, Vol. 62, No.2, June 1972, p. 194.

[26] For a delineation and characteristics of the region see: Jean Gottmann, Megalopolis, New York: The Twentieth Century Fund, 1961.

[27] James E. Vance, op. cit., p. 193.

[28] Ibid, p. 193.

[29] Marion Clawson, Suburban Land Conversion in the United States: An Economic and Governmental Process, Baltimore: The Johns Hopkins Press, 1971, (Published for Resources for the Future, Inc.), p. 53.

[30] Ibid, p. 53.

[31] Ibid, p. 54.

[32] For research trends in settlement geography see: Clyde F. Kohn, et. al, "Settlement Geography," James E. Preston and Clarence F. Jones (Editors), American Geography: Inventory and Prospect, Syracuse and Syracuse University Press, 1954. (Published for the Association of American Geographers), pp. 124-166.

[33] For a definition of the "Bluegrass Region" see: "Kentucky's Bluegrass-The Study Area", p. 11.

[34] Oscar Rucker, Jr., "A Geographic Study of Rural Settlement Clusters in Madison County, Kentucky," Master's Thesis Department of Geography, University of Kentucky, 1967.

[35] Lexington-Fayette Planning Commission, Rural Settlements Housing Study, Lexington, 1971.

[36] Peter Craig Smith, "Negro Hamlets and Gentlemen Farms: A Dichotomous Rural Settlement Pattern in Kentucky's Bluegrass Region, " Ph.D. Dissertation, Department of Geography, University of Kentucky, 1972.

[37] Thomas P. Field, Mobile Homes of Kentucky and the Lexington Hexagon: A Study in Areal Distribution. Kentucky Study Series #5, Lexington Department of Geography and Fayette County Geographical Society, University of Kentucky, 1971.

[38]Phillips, op. cit.

[39]Ibid., p. 15.

[40]Glenn T. Trewartha, "The Unincorporated Hamlet," Annals of the Association of American Geographers, Volume 33, 1943, p. 37.

[41]Rucker, op. cit., p. 22.

[42]Lexington-Fayette County Planning Commission, op. cit., p. 30.

[43]Smith, op. cit., p. 4.

[44]Ibid., p. 10.

[45]Ibid., p. 44.

[46]Ibid., p. 44.

[47]Ibid., p. 77.

[48]Ibid., p. 78.

[49]Much of Field's study is omitted from this brief review, since it is not directly relevant here.

[50]Field, op. cit., p. 39.

[51]Ibid., p. 29.

[52]Ibid., p. 45.

[53]Phillips, op. cit., p. 3.

[54]Ibid., p. 74.

[55]Ibid., p. vi.

[56]Ibid., p. vii.

[57]Ibid., p. 47.

[58]Kentucky Department of Highways, Division of Planning and United States Department of Commerce, Bureau of Public Roads, General Highway Maps of Anderson, Bourbon, Clark, Fayette, Jessamine, Madison, and Woodford Counties, Frankfort, Kentucky: Kentucky Department of Transportation, 1974.

[59]Rucker, op. cit., p. 7, differentiates between linear "without intersection"-"with intersection" and "with bends."

Chapter 2

[1] John Fraser Hart, "Urban Encroachment on Rural Areas, The Geographical Review, Vol. 66, No. 1, January, 1976, p.4.

[2] Ibid., p. 6.

[3] Ibid., p. 9.

[4] Ibid., p. 15.

[5] "Basic Statistics of the National Inventory of Soil and Water Conservation Needs," U.S. Department of Agriculture, Statistical Bulletin 317, Washington, D.C., August 1962, and Basic Statistics--"National Inventory of Soil and Water Conservation Needs, 1967," U.S. Department of Agriculture, Statistical Bulletin 461, Washington, D.C., 1971.

[6] A. Allen Schmid, Converting Land from Rural to Urban Uses, Washington, D.C.: Resources of the Future Inc., 1968, p. 8.

[7] Ibid., p. 14.

[8] Ibid., p. 22.

[9] Ibid., p. 25.

[10] A. Allen Schmid, "Suburban Land Appreciation and Public Policy," American Institute of Planners Journal, Vol. 36, January 1970, p. 40.

[11] For a list containing monographs, journal articles and thesis see "Selected References" in Traffic Quarterly Vol. 23, No. 4, October 1969, pp. 631-632.

[12] Edward J. Kaiser and Shirley F. Weiss, "Decision Agent Models of the Residential Development Process -- A Review of Recent Research, "Traffic Quarterly Vol. 23, No. 4, October 1969, 597-632.

[13] Edward J. Kaiser and Shirley F. Weiss, "Public Policy and the Residential Development Process" in Larry S. Bourne (Editor) Internal Structure of the City, Readings on Space and Environment, New York, Oxford University Press, 1971, p. 189.

[14] Ibid., p. 189.

[15] See John F. Smith, "Toward a Theory of Landowner Behavior on the Urban Periphery," 1966 Thesis: University of North Carolina; and Edward J. Kaiser, Ronald W. Massie, Shirley F. Weiss and John E. Smith, "Predicting the Behavior of Predevelopment Landowner in the Urban Fringe," Journal of the American Institute of Planners, Vol. 34, No. 5, September 1968, pp. 328-333.

[16] Kaiser and Weiss, "Decision Agent Models..." op. cit., p. 603.

[17] Ibid., p. 604.

[18] Ibid., p. 608.

[19] Michael A. Goldberg, "Residential Develper Be havior: Some Empirical Findings" Appraisal Institute Magazine, Vol. 19, Book 4, Winter 1975, p. 11.

[20] Ibid., p. 13.

[21] George A McBridge and Marion Clawson, "Negotiation and Land Conversion," Journal of the American Institute of Planners, Vol. 36, No. 1, January 1970, p. 28.

[22] Information which would identify an individual developer is not presented here.

[23] Land Subdivision Regulations, Lexington, Kentucky: Lexington-Fayette County Planning Commission, 1969, p. 6-3.

[24] Kaiser and Weiss, "Public Policy..." op. cit., p. 191.

[25] Ibid., p. 191.

[26] Ibid., p. 191.

[27] Ibid., p. 191.

[28] Ibid., p. 192.

[29] Ibid., p. 192.

[30] Kaiser and Weiss, "Decision Agent Models..." op. cit., p. 630.

[31] Ibid., p. 630.

Chapter 3

[1]Kentucky Department of Highways, Division of Planning and United States Department of Commerce, Bureau of Public Roads, General Highway Maps of Bourbon, Clark, Fayette, Jessamine, Madison, Scott, and Woodford counties, Frankfort, Kentucky, Kentucky Department of Transportation, 1974.

[2]The quality rating of exurbs is discussed in section two of this chapter.

[3]Phillip D. Phillips, Exurban Commuters in the Kentucky Bluegrass Region, Lexington: Center for Real Estate and Land Use Analysis, Monograph #5, 1976, p. 29.

[4]Minimum lot size of 10 acres in Fayette county and 5 acres in the counties adjacent to Fayette, for a single family dwelling on septic tank came into existence after 1969.

[5]Phillip D. Phillips, "Commuting and Energy Consumption in Kentucky", Focus on Kentucky, Vol. 2, No. 10, November 1974, pp. 2-3 & 7.

[6]Ibid., p. 7.

[7]The qualitative rating of the exurbs does not mean that the "quality of life" is inferred.

[8]The Urban Service area concept was adopted by Fayette county in 1958. It now includes 74.4 square miles, representing 26 percent of the county's total area of 283 square miles. For more details see Lexington Fayette County Planning Commission, A Growing Community, pp. 30-31.

Chapter 4

[1]See Auguste C. Spectorsky, The Exurbanites. Philadelphia: J.P. Lippincott Co., 1955.

[2]Sylvia F. Fava, "Beyond Suburbia" The Annals of the
Academy of Political and Social Science, 422 (November,
1975).

[3]The three indicators selcted have consistently shown
to be associated with the SES dimension, see for example:
Eshref Shevky and Marilyn Williams, The Social Areas of
Los Angeles, Berkeley. The University of California Press,
1944; Eshref Shevky and Wendell Bell, The Social Area
Analysis, Stanford: Stanford University Press, 1955, and
Brian J. L. Berry and Frank E. Horton, Geographic Perspectives
on Urban Systems, Englewood Cliffs, N.J.: Prentice Hall,
Inc., 1970, pp. 378-382.

[4]op. cit.

[5]U.S. Bureau of the Census, Census of Population: 1970
General Social and Economic Characteristics, Final Report
PC(1)-C19 Kentucky, Washington, D.C.: U.S. Government
Printing Office, 1972.

[6]U.S. Census of the Population, Classification Index
of Industries and Occupation, Washington, D.C.: U.S.
Government Printing Office, 1971.

[7]Marion Clawson, Suburban Land Conversion in the
United States: An Economic and Governmental Process,
Baltimore: John Hopkins Press, 1971.

[8]The CRV is computed by dividing the standard deviation
by the mean and multiplying the product by 100. See John
H. Mueller, Karl F. Schuessler, Herbert L. Costner, Statistical Reasoning in Sociology (Second Edition). Boston:
Houghton Mifflin, Co., 1970.

[9]See Phillips op. cit. for a discussion of the "push"
factors which cause an outward migration from the city and
the "pull" factors which make exurban areas attractive.

[10]Sylvia F. Fava, op. cit., p. 10.

[11]Sylvia F. Fava, ibid., p. 10.

[12]For a description of the information sources used
for residential search in an urban area see John S. Adams,
"Directional Bias in Intra-Urban Migration," Economic
Geography, Vol. 25, No. 4, October, 1969, pp. 302-323.

Chapter 5

[1]Brian J.L. Berry, The Human Consequences of Urbanization. New York: St. Martins Press, 1973, p. 43.

[2]The distance traveled by urban dwellers is based after Phillip D. Phillips, Exurban Commuters in the Kentucky Bluegrass Region. Monograph #5, Lexington: Center for Real Estate and Land Use Analysis, University of Kentucky, 1967, p. 29.

[3]BGADD has as its general purpose the promotion of economic development and the establishment of a framework for joint federal, state and local efforts directed towards providing basic services, facilities, and opportunities essential to the social, economic and physical development of the district. For more details see Bluegrass Area Development District, Preliminary Land Use Plan, 1972.

[4]See Phillip D. Phillips, op. cit., for a discussion of selected Bluegrass communities, pp. 50-51.

[5]Bluegrass Area Development District. Progress Report: Regional Housing Activities, mimeo, June, 1975.

115

EXURBS WITH CONVENTIONAL DWELLINGS

	Name	County	Number of Dwellings	Rating[1]
1.	Apple Hill Estates	Fayette	5	1
2.	Avon Estates	Fayette	44	2
3.	Barckley Estates	Jessamine	14	2
4.	Bryan Estates	Jessamine	10	3
5.	Bird Acres	Jessamine	13	3
6.	Boone Village	Madison	60	3
7.	Brocklyn Estates	Madison	56	3
8.	Cedar Hills	Jessamine	50	1
9.	Cherrywood Estates	Jessamine	14	2
10.	Circle Five Farm Estates	Fayette	5	1
11.	Clays Ferry Estates	Madison	17	3
12.	Colonial Estates	Jessamine	10	3
13.	Country Club Heights	Madison	47	2
14.	Crestview	Madison	33	3
15.	Deacon Hills	Madison	200	1
16.	Eastpoint Subdivision	Fayette	37	2
17.	Emerald Hill Farm Estates	Fayette	3	1
18.	Estonia Estates	Madison	48	3
19.	Etterwood Estates	Scott	52	3
20.	Executive Park	Madison	20	3
21.	Fieldcrest	Bourbon	25	3

[1] Each of the exurbs was rated on a scale of 1 thru 6. The criteria for rating are outlined in Table 11.

APPENDIX I (Continued)

	Name	County	Number of Dwellings	Rating[1]
22.	Fountain Park	Madison	7	3
23.	Gaybourne	Woodford	43	2
24.	Glenhaven Colony	Woodford	27	2
25.	Greenbrier Estates	Fayette	89	1
26.	Greenbrier Estates	Madison	32	3
27.	Greenland Estates	Fayette	5	1
28.	Hickory Hills	Madison	12	1
29.	Hillcrest	Madison	129	2
30.	Hilltop Meadows	Woodford	20	3
31.	Idylwyld Subdivision	Madison	19	2
32.	Lakewood	Madison	24	2
33.	Lancaster Woods	Madison	16	1
34.	Lancelot Estates	Scott	84	3
35.	Longview Estates	Scott	15	2
36.	Lyndale	Clark	116	3
37.	Lynmar	Bourbon	12	3
38.	Madison Village	Madison	15	3
39.	Marbletop Subdivision	Jessamine	36	3
40.	Meadowview	Madison	30	3
41.	Milford Estates	Madison	31	2
42.	Moon Lake Estates	Scott	43	3
43.	Mountain View	Madison	30	3

118

	Name	County	Number of Dwellings	Rating
44.	Oak Grove Estates	Jessamine	3	2
45.	Paddock Place	Woodford	183	3
46.	Robinsville	Madison	37	3
47.	Rolling Hills	Fayette	35	2
48.	Rose Hills	Madison	9	1
49.	Shethland	Woodford	42	3
50.	Spindletop Estates	Fayette	48	2
51.	Stonecrest	Clark	3	3
52.	Stonehedge	Scott	10	3
53.	Sycamore Estates	Woodford	287	2
54.	Turner Estates	Fayette	4	1
55.	Verna Hills	Clark	41	3
56.	Village Square	Madison	36	3
57.	Vincewood Estates	Jessamine	9	1
58.	Wayland Heights	Clark	40	3
59.	Wellesley Heights	Fayette	27	1
60.	Westchester Manor	Clark	9	2
61.	Westmead	Clark	23	3
62.	Westmoreland Estates	Fayette	82	1
63.	Woodford Estates	Clark	24	2
64.	White Hall Manor[2]	Madison	68	3 and 4

[2] This exurb has 39 conventional dwellings and 29 mobile homes which are rated as 3 and 4, respectively.

119

APPENDIX II

EXURBS WITH MOBILE HOMES

	Name	County	Number of Dwellings	Rating[1]
1.	Ash Grove East	Jessamine	41	5
2.	Ash Grove Pike	Jessamine	6	6
3.	Ash Grove West	Jessamine	31	5
4.	Bethlehem	Bourbon	13	5
5.	Bluegrass	Scott	10	6
6.	Bond's	Clark	21	5
7.	Bourbon	Woodford	27	4
8.	Country Living	Bourbon	56	4
9.	Cool Breeze	Jessamine	41	6
10.	Co-Z	Jessamine	48	5
11.	Eden Heights	Jessamine	24	6
12.	Forest Grove	Clark	12	5
13.	Green Meadows	Scott	46	5
14.	Interstate	Scott	26	5
15.	Judianna	Clark	41	4
16.	Kerr	Bourbon	25	5
17.	Locustwood	Fayette	93	4
18.	Lee's Park	Scott	23	5
19.	Leedean's Mobile Home Ests.	Jessamine	30	5

[1]Each of the exurbs was rated on a scale of 1 thru 6. The criteria for rating are outlined in Table 11.

	Name	County	Number of Dwellings	Rating[1]
20.	Marina's	Clark	10	5
21.	Moller	Jessamine	17	5
22.	Mason's	Woodford	9	4
23.	Noland's Ash Grove Estates	Jessamine	102	4
24.	Paddock	Scott	9	6
25.	Ponderosa	Scott	46	5
26.	Rockwell	Clark	35	4
27.	Red Oak	Jessamine	13	5
28.	Spindletop	Scott	154	4
29.	Smitts	Bourbon	80	6
30.	Spurlin's	Madison	127	5
31.	Steel's	Woodford	38	5
32.	Tates Creek Estates	Jessamine	102	5
33.	Truck Stop	Scott	10	6
34.	Tuttle's	Bourbon	19	4
35.	Windmill	Jessamine	58	5
36.	York Towne	Clark	85	4

---

[1] Each of the exurbs was rated on a scale of 1 thru 6. The criteria for rating are outlined in Table 11.

APPENDIX III: EXURBAN RESIDENTIAL PREFERENCE INTERVIEW SCHEDULE

Date of Interview _____ Interviewer _____ Exurb _____ Sample # _____

I. RESIDENT FAMILY MEMBERS: Put in the head of household first, then the homemaker and children.

Relation to Head[1]	Sex[2]	Age	Marital Status[3]	Occupation or Grade, If in School	Job Status[4]	Highest Edn. If not in School	Place of Work or Name of School[5]	Travel Time to Work or School	Transportation to Work/ School[6]
--	--	-- --	--	-- --	--	-- --	-- --	-- --	--
1.									
2.									
3.									
4.									
5.									
6.									
7.									
8.									

1. Relation to Head: 1-Husband, 2-Wife, 3-Son, 4-Daughter, 5-Grandparent, 6-Other.
2. Sex: 1-Male, 2-Female.
3. Marital Status: 1-Single, 2-Married, 3-Separated, 4-Divorced, 5-Widowed.
4. Job Status: 1-Full-Time, 2-Part-time, 3-Unemployed, 4-Retired.
5. 21-Public School, 22-Private or Parochial School

EDN CODE: 21-1 to 8 grade; 22-some high school; 23-high school grad; 24-some college; 25-Bachelor's degree; 26-some graduate school; 27-Masters degree; 28-doctoral/professional.

# of Non-Resident Family _____ Members.

6. 1-Auto; 2-Carpool; 3-Bus; 4-Walk; 5-Other.

COMMENTS: _____

122

II. COMMUTING

- a. How many cars does your family own? _____

- b. (If interviewee does not carpool) Would you carpool if you could find someone with a work place and time the same as yours? 1-YES___ 2-NO___ 3-Undecided___

III. RESIDENTIAL

- a. How long have you lived at this residence? ____years. [If 9+, code as 9]

- b. Was this residence previously occupied? 1-Yes___ 2-No___ .

- If yes, how old is this residence? _____ years.
- If NOT, which one of the following explains your situation.

    1. ___ the house was custom built on a vacant lot.

    2. ___ the house was built from alternate plans offered by the builder.

    3. ___ the house was under construction when you saw it.

    4. ___ the house was ready to occupy when you saw it.

  c. Please rate the following in terms of importance as a reason for living in this subdivision. (Place a check mark in the appropriate column)

	Not Important (1)	Moderately Important (2)	Very Important (3)
- Cost of housing			
- Close to work			
- Open space			
- Good Schools			
- Friendly Neighbors			
- Close to Nature			
- Low taxes			
- Peaceful, quiet surroundings			
- Safe, low crime area			

[Code missing values as 9]

-- d. Here is a list of some of the features which are important to people when they look for a place to live. Which two of the features were most important to you (indicate 1 and 2)

1. ___ closet space   4. ___ number of bathrooms   7. ___ garage or other parking

2. ___ floor plan   5. ___ size of rooms

3. ___ number of bedrooms 6. ___ storage area   8. ___ size of lot

                                                           9. ___ type of building materials used

— e. Which one of the following describes your childhood residence?

	HUSBANDS	WIVES
1. a rural farm house (county, state)	_____	_____
2. a coutryside subdivision (county,state)	_____	_____
3. a small town (name)	_____	_____
4. a city suburb (suburb,city)	_____	_____
5. a city (name)	_____	_____

— f. Which one of the following describes the most recent previous residence?

	HUSBANDS	WIVES
1. a rural farm house (county/ state)	_____	_____
2. a countryside subdivision (county,state)	_____	_____
3. a small town (name)	_____	_____
4. a city suburb (suburb,city)	_____	_____
5. a city (name)	_____	_____

- g. Do you wish this subdivision 1. ___ were smaller in size, 2.___ to remain the same in size, 3. ___ to be larger than its present size.

- h. Do you feel your present lot size is 1.___ too big; 2.___about right;3.___ 3.___too small.

- i. Are you satisfied with the job the developer has done? 1. Yes___ 2. No___.

In what way_____

- j. All in all would you say that you like this neighborhood better or your old neighborhood? 1. ___ new neighborhood 2. ___about the same 3. ___ old neighborhood.

Why do you say so?_____

- k. How did you come to know about this subdivision:
  1. ___ thru a friend   4.___ from an ad in newspaper, radio, TV

  2. ___ thru a realtor   5. ___ other (specify)_____

  3. ___ from driving around

- l. Do you own or rent this house? 1.___own   2.___ rent.

124

---.- m. If OWNER... What is the amount of monthly mortgage you pay?_____

    1. Paid up   4. $200-299   7. $500 and over
    2. Less than $100   5. $300-399
    3. $100-$199   6. $400-499

   n. IF RENTER. . . What is the amount of monthly rent you pay?_____

    1. Under $50   4. $150-199   7. Over $300
    2. $50-$99   5. $200-249
    3. $100-149   6. $250-300

---.-- IF OWNER . . . Could you tell me what the present value of the home is--
i.e., about what would it bring if you sold it?_____

    1. Below $5000   7, $30,000-34,999   13. 70,000-79,999
    2. $5000-9,999   8. $35,000-39,999   14. $80,000-89,999
    3. $10,000-14,999   9. $40,000-44,999   15. $90,000-99,999
    4. $15,000-19,999 10. $45,000-49,999 16. $100,000-149,999
    5. $20,000-24,999 11. $50,000-59,999 17. $150,000-199,999
    6. $25,000-29,999 12. $60,000-69,999 18. $200,000 and over.

IV. UTILITY SERVICES

- a. Are you on 1. private sewage system____   2.septic tank____

- b. What kind of heating do you have? 1.electric heat___ 2. natural gas heat___
                                3. bottle gas heat____.

- c. Is your garbage collection provided thru:

    1.____ a nearby urban service area   3.____ public dumpsters

    2.____ a private contractor   4.____ is not provided

V. SHOPPING

   a. Where do you usually go for the following:

  - - Groceries   _____

  - - Furniture   _____

  - - Appliances   _____

  - - Clothing   _____

  - - Banking   _____

  - - Professional Ser-
     vices (Doctor,
     Dentist, Lawyer) _____

  - - Church   _____

- b. If a new shopping center were to develop within walking distance of this subdivision, would you 1. go along with it___,2.object to it___, or 3. don't care
one way ot the other____.

IV. INCOME

- - Circle the letter that would describe your total family income before taxes last year:

01. Under $2,999

02. $3,000 - $4,999

03. $5,000 - $7,499

04. $7,500 - $9,999

05. $10,000 - $14,999

06. $15,000 - $19,999

07. $20,000 - $24,999

08. $25,000 - $29,999

09. $30,000 - 34,999

10. $35,000 - $39,999

11. $40,000 -$44,999

12. $45,000 -$49,999

13. Over $50,000

- Number of wage earners

-- Number of family members depending on the above income

BIBLIOGRAPHY

ARTICLES

Adams, John S. "Directional Bias in Intra-Urban Migration." Economic Geography, Vol. 45, No. 4 (October 1969), 302-23.

Adams, John S. "Residential Structure of Midwestern Cities." Annals of the Association of American Geographers, Vol. 60, No. 1 (March 1970), 37-62.

Bladen, Wilford A. "Evolution of a Compage: The Case of Lexington, Kentucky." Research paper presented at the Annual Meeting of the Kentucky Academy of Science, Richmond, Kentucky, (November 1970).

Borchert, John R. "American Metropolitan Evolution." Geographical Review, Vol. 57, No. 4 (October 1970) 301-23.

Clark, Collin. "Urban Population Densities." Journal of the Royal Statistical Society, Vol. 114, Part 4, (1951), 490-96.

Egan, Richard. "How Ya Gonna Keep 'Em in Metropolis After They've Seen the Countryside?" The National Observer, (May 31, 1975).

Egerton, J. W. "The Problem of Rurban Properties", Appraisal Institute Magazine, Vol. 17, Book 2 (Summer 1973), 31-37.

Fava, Sylvia F. "Beyond Suburbia." The Annals of the American Academy of Political and Social Science, 442, (November 1975), 10-24.

Goldberg, Michael A. "Residential Developer Behavior: Some Empirical Findings." Appraisal Institute Magazine, Vol. 19, Book 4, (Winter 1975), 11-14.

Hart, John Fraser. "Urban Encroachment of Rural Areas." The Geographical Review, Vol. 66, No. 1, (January 1976), 1-17.

Hughes, James W. "Dilemmas of Suburbanization and Growth Controls." The Annals of the American Academy of Political and Social Science, 422, (November 1975), 61-76.

Isberg, Gunnar. "Controlling Growth in the Urban Fringe." Current Municipal Problems, Vol. 16, (1974-75), 86-104.

Johnston, R. J. "The Location of High Status Residential Areas", Geografiska Annaler, Vol. 48B, No. 1, (January 1966), 25-35.

Kaiser, Edward J. and Weiss, Shirley F. "Decision Agent Models of the Residential Development of the Residential Development Process -- A Review of Recent Research." Traffic Quarterly, Vol. 23, No. 4, (October 1969).

Masotti, Louis H. "Preface." The Annals of the American Academy of Political and Social Science, 422, (November 1975), vii.

McBride, George A. "Negotiation and Land Conversion." Journal of the American Institute of Planners, Vol. 36, No. 1, (January 1970), 22-37.

Moriarty, Barry M. "Socioeconomic Status and Residential Locational Choice", Environment and Behavior, Vol. 6, No. 4, (December 1974), 448-69.

Myers, R. B. and Beegle T. A. "Delineation and Analysis of the Rural Urban Fringe" Applied Anthropology, Vol. 6 (1947), 14-22.

Newling, Bruce. "The Spatial Variation of Urban Population Densities." Geographical Review, Vol. 59, No. 2, (April 1969), 242-52.

Pearson, Norman. "The Effect of Urbanization on Agricultural Land" Appraisal Institute Magazine, Vol. 16, Book 3, (Autumn 1972), 25-34.

Phillips, Phillip D. "Commuting and Energy Consumption in Kentucky", Focus on Kentucky, Vol. 2, No. 2, (November 1974).

Pryor, Robin J. "Delineating the Outer Suburbs and the Urban Fringe", Geografiska Annaler, Vol. 51B, No. 1, (January 1969), 33-38.

Schmid, A. Allen. "Suburban Land Appreciation and Public
    Policy." American Institute of Planners Journal,
    Vol. 36, No. 1, (January 1970), 38-43.

Slater, Ronald W. and McGonigaly, Marvin A. "Mobile Home
    Park Development - A Residential Revolution",
    Appraisal Institute Magazine, Vol. 17, Book 2,
    (Summer 1973) 12-20.

Trewartha, Glenn T. "The Unincorporated Hamlet." Annals
    of the Association of American Geographers,
    Volume 33, (1943), 37.

Vance, James E. Jr. "California and the Search for the
    Ideal." Annals of the Association of American
    Geographers, Vol. 62, No. 2, (June 1972), 185-210.

Wehrwein, G. S. "The Rural Urban Fringe", Economic
    Geography, Vol. 18 (1942), 217-28.

Weiss, Shirley F. and Smith, John E. "Predicting the
    Behavior of Predevelopment Landwoner in the Urban
    Fringe." Journal of the American Institute of
    Planners, Vol. 34, No. 5, (September 1968).

BOOKS AND MONOGRAPHS

Berry, Brian J. L. "Population Growth in the Daily Urban
    System of the United States, 1980-2000." U.S.,
    Commission on Population Growth and the American
    Future, Population, Distribution and Policy, 1974.

_____, The Human Consequences of Urbanization. New York:
    St. Martin's Press, 1973.

Bluegrass Area Development District, Bluegrass Area De-
    velopment District Regional Comprehensive Water and
    Sewer Plan, Lexington, Ky.: Bluegrass Area De-
    velopment District, Inc., 1973.

Clawson, Marion. Suburban Land Conversion in the United
    States: An Economic and Governmental Process.
    Baltimore: The Johns Hopkins Press, 1971, (Published
    for Resources for the Future, Inc.)

Environmental Protection Agency. Control of Erosion and and Sediment Deposition from Construction of Highways and Land Development. Washington, D.C., 1971.

Field, Thomas P. Mobile Homes of Kentucky and the Lexington Hexagon: A Study in Areal Distribution. Kentucky Study Series #5, Lexington Department of Geography and Fayette County Geographical Society, University of Kentucky, 1971.

Gottman, Jean. Megalopolis. New York: The Twentieth Fund, 1961.

Gottman, Jean and Harper, Robert A. Metropolis on the Move: Geographers Look at Urban Sprawl, New York: John Wiley and Sons, Inc., 1967.

Johnson, James Henry (Editor), Suburban Growth: Geographical Processes at the Fage of the Western City, New York: John Wiley and Sons, Inc., 1974.

Kaiser, Edward J. and Weiss, Shirley F. "Public Policy and the Residential Development Process." Larry S. Bourne (Editor) Internal Structure of the City, Readings on Space and Environment, New York, Oxford University Press, 1971.

Kohn, Clyde F., et al, "Settlement Geography," James E. Preston and Clarence F. Jones (Editors), American Geography: Inventory and Prospect, Syracuse and Syracuse University Press, 1954. (Published for the Association of American Geographers).

Muller, John H., Schuessler, Karl F., and Costner, Herbert L., Statistical Reasoning in Sociology (Second Edition), Boston: Houghton Mifflin Co., 1970.

Nie, Norman H., Bent, Dale H., and Hull, C. Hadlai. Statistical Package for the Social Sciences (Second Edition) New York: McGraw-Hill, 1975.

Northam, Ray M. Urban Geography, New York: John Wiley and Sons, Inc., 1975.

Phillips, Phillips D. Exurban Commuters in the Kentucky Bluegrass Region. Lexington: Center for Real Estate and Land Use Analysis, Monograph #5, 1976.

Raitz, Karl B. "The Bluegrass" in P. P. Karan (Editor)
    Kentucky: A Regional Geography, Dubuque, Iowa:
    Kendall/Hunt Publishing Company, 1973.

Schmid, A. Allen. Converting Land from Rural to Urban
    Uses. Washington, D.C.: Resources of the Future,
    Inc., 1968.

Spectorsky, Auguste C. The Exurbanites. Philadelphia:
    J. P. Lippincott Co., 1955.

Webster's New World Dictionary, Second College Edition,
    New York: The World Publishing Company, 1972.

Whittlesey, Derwent. "The Regional Concept and the
    Regional Method." James E. Preston and Clarance F.
    Jones (Editors), American Geography: Inventory and
    Prospect, Syracuse, N.Y.: Syracuse University
    Press, 1954.

Yeates, Maurice H. and Garner, Barry J. "Evolution of the
    Urban Pattern." The North American City. New York:
    Harper and Row, Publishers, 1976. Second Edition.

GOVERNMENT DOCUMENTS

Lexington-Fayette County Planning Commission. Land Sub-
    division Regulations. Lexington, Kentucky: 1969.

Lexington-Fayette Planning Commission, Rural Settlements
    Housing Study. Lexington, Kentucky, 1971.

U.S. Bureau of the Census, Census of Population, 1970,
    Detailed Characteristics, Final Report PC (1) - 01
    United States Summary, Washington, D.C.: U.S.
    Government Printing Office, 1973.

U.S. Department of Agriculture. "Basic Statistics of the
    National Inventory of Soil and Water Conservation
    Needs." U.S. Department of Agriculture, Statistical
    Bulletin 317, Washington, D.C., August 1962.

U.S. Department of Agriculture. "Basic Statistics of the
    National Inventory of Siol and Water Conservation
    Needs, 1967. U.S. Department of Agriculture,
    Statistical Bulletin 461, Washington, D.C., 1971.

MAPS

Kentucky Department of Highways, Division of Planning,
    General Highway Map, Anderson County, Kentucky,
    Kentucky Department of Highways, Frankfort, Kentucky,
    1974.

_____, General Highway Map, Bourbon County, Kentucky,
    Kentucky Department of Highways, Frankfort, Kentucky,
    1974.

_____, General Highway Map, Clark County, Kentucky,
    Kentucky Department of Highways, Frankfort, Kentucky,
    1974.

_____, General Highway Map, Fayette County, Kentucky,
    Kentucky Department of Highways, Frankfort, Kentucky,
    1974.

_____, General Highway Map, Jessamine County, Kentucky,
    Kentucky Department of Highways, Frankfort, Kentucky,
    1974.

_____, General Highway Map, Madison County, Kentucky,
    Kentucky Department of Highways, Frankfort, Kentucky,
    1974.

_____, General Highway Map, Woodford County, Kentucky,
    Kentucky Department of Highways, Frankfort, Kentucky,
    1974.

THESES AND DISSERTATIONS

Rucker, Oscar Jr. "A Geographic Study of Rural Settlement
    Clusters in Madison County, Kentucky." Master's
    Thesis, Department of Geography, University of
    Kentucky, 1967.

Smith, John E. "Toward a Theory of Landowner Behavior on
    the Urban Periphery." Master's Thesis, University of
    North Carolina, 1966.

Smith, Peter Craig. "Negro Hamlets and Gentlemen Farms:
    A Dichotomous Rural Settlement Patter in Kentucky's
    Bluegrass Region." Ph.D. Dissertation, Department of
    Geography, University of Kentucky, 1972.

132

ABOUT THE AUTHOR

The author was born on January 26, 1945 in Nairobi, Kenya, where he received his primary and secondary education; and two years of college. He came to the United States in December 1965, receiving scholarships from Eastern Oregon College and Phelps-Stokes Foundation, to attend EasternOregon College, La Grande, Oregon, from where he graduated with a B.S. degree in 1968. He obtained his M.A. and Ph.D. degrees from the University of Kentucky. He is presently an Associate Professor of Sociology at Kentucky State University. He lives in Lexington, Kentucky, with his wife, Mrudula, daughter Alpa, and son Anuj.

Dinker I. Patel
January 1980